edexcel
advancing learning, changing lives

Edexcel

Functional Skills

Eng

Written by Clare

Consultants: Jen

Leve

A PEARSON COMPANY

Heinemann is an imprint of Pearson Education Limited, a company incorporated in England and Wales, having its registered office at Edinburgh Gate, Harlow, Essex, CM20 2JE. Registered company number: 872828

www.pearsonschoolsandfecolleges.co.uk

Heinemann is a registered trademark of Pearson Education Limited

Text © Pearson Education Limited, 2010

First published 2010

12
10 9 8 7 6 5 4 3

British Library Cataloguing in Publication Data
A catalogue record for this book is available from the British Library.

ISBN 978 1 846 90693 0

Produced by Pearson Education Ltd, 2010
Designed and produced by Kamae Design, Oxford
Original illustrations © Pearson Education, 2010
Cover design by Pete Stratton
Picture research by Caitlin Swain
Cover photo © Shutterstock images
Printed in Malaysia, CTP-KHL

Acknowledgements

The author and publisher would like to thank the following individuals and organisations for permission to reproduce photographs:

Nathan Benn/Alamy; David R. Frazier Photolibrary, Inc./Alamy; Cusp/Superstock Ltd; Image Source/Image Source Ltd; Yadid Levy/ Alamy; Keith Morris/Alamy; Daniel Atkin/Alamy; Mike Marsland/ WireImage/Getty Images; Clandestini/WestEnd61/Rex Features; Cycling Images; Evan Agostini/Associated Press/Press Association Images; New Zealand stock/Alamy; speedpix/Alamy; Janine Wiedel Photolibrary/Alamy; P. Broze/Getty Images; Clark Wiseman/Pearson Education; Ryan McVay/Getty Images; Sipa Press/Rex Features; Flirt /Superstock Ltd; Jose Luis Pelaez, Inc./Corbis UK Ltd; Adrian Sherratt/Alamy; Richard Gardette/Corbis UK Ltd; Brian Harris/ Alamy; Jim West/Alamy; Blend Images/Alamy; Peter Titmuss/ Alamy; PCL/Alamy; age fotostock/Superstock Ltd; Hufton + Crow/ Photolibrary Group; Jeffrey Blackler/Alamy; Kristy-Anne Glubish/ Design Pics Inc./Rex Features; Peter M Corr/Alamy; Zooid Pictures; Onne Van Der Wal/Corbis UK Ltd; Mark Bassett/Pearson Education; Stephane Cardinale/People Avenue/Corbis UK Ltd; Brian Rasic/Rex Features; Radius Images/Alamy; Tim Pannell/Corbis UK Ltd; Iain Laskey / Alamy

The author and publisher would like to thank the following individuals and organisations for permission to reproduce copyright material:

Theme Park – UK logo. Copyright © www.themeparks-uk.com. Reproduced by permission of Theme Parks – UK; Adventure Island Logo. Reproduced with permission of Adventure Island, a member of the Stockvale Group; Camelot Theme Park logo. Reproduced by permission of Camelot Theme Park; Nokia Phone 1661 image. Reproduced by permission of Nokia Corporation; Safety leaflet: *Your Guide to keeping your home safe*. Published by Home Office Communications Directorate, June 2002; Extract from Universal Declaration of Human Rights Abridged for Youth; Panelbase & Paid surveys for Teens – Get paid to be young from http://www.teenpaidsurveys.co.uk. Reproduced by permission of Teen Paid Surveys; Extract from Talk Football website; Extract from rugbyunionrules.com; Extracts from the Laterooms.com website; Extracts and logo from the Fifteen website. Reproduced with permission of the Jamie Oliver Foundation; Extract from "Louis' story" found on the Shelter website; Extract from 'Give Your Skin A Break This Holiday' leaflet from the Cosmetic Toiletry and Perfume Association and The British Skin Foundation. Reproduced with permission. Reproduced from the CTPA consumer website www.thefactsabout.co.uk – see 'Stay sun safe'; I want one of those logo and web page. Reproduced with permission of I want one of those; The Ryedale Rumble from Cycling Weekly. Copyright © Cycling Weekly / IPC+ Syndication, used with permission; Santa letter marketing advert from the Carphone Warehouse; 'Airbrushing of photos should be banned, Liberal Democrats say' by Rosa Prince. Copyright © 3rd August 2009, The Telegraph. Reproduced by permission of The Telegraph; 'Lighten up - Kate Moss is right' by Eleanor Mills. Copyright © The Times, 22 November 2009 / nisyndication.com. Reproduced by permission; Government Leaflet regarding consumer fraud reporting; 'Lessons in being a parent at just 14' by Laura Clark. Daily Mail 4/01/2010. Reproduced by permission of Solo Syndication; Quote from JP, Teenage Dad. Based on video material from DVD (Dads Matter Too) online about Invisible fathers / Fatherhood Institute. Reproduced with permission of U Too; Extract from eDofE: *Future, Present & Annual Review*. Used with permission; CitizenCard, Copyright © CitizenCard Limited. Reproduced with permission of CitizenCard Limited; Card samples from National Identity Cards; Sample Travel Cards produced by STA Travel.

Every effort has been made to contact copyright holders of material reproduced in this book. Any omissions will be rectified in subsequent printings if notice is given to the publishers.

Thanks to the staff and students at Thames Christian College for their invaluable help with research and exemplar students' work.

Websites
The websites used in this book were correct and up-to-date at the time of publication. It is essential for tutors to preview each website before using it in class so as to ensure that the URL is still accurate, relevant and appropriate. We suggest that tutors bookmark useful websites and consider enabling students to access them through the school/college intranet.

Contents

Introduction

Welcome to Edexcel Functional Skills English. We've worked hard to plan this course to make sure you are fully prepared for your Functional Skills English assessments.

Functional English aims to ensure that you are confident and capable when using the skills of speaking, listening, reading and writing. It will equip you to communicate effectively, adapting to a range of audiences and contexts.

Good luck with your studies. We hope you achieve a good Level 2 Pass.

Clare Constant
Head of English
and Literacy

Keith Washington
Chief Examiner
(pilot scheme)

How is this book structured?

This book is divided into three learning sections:

▶ Reading
▶ Speaking, listening and communication
▶ Writing

These correspond to the three areas you will be assessed on for Functional Skills English.

Each section is broken down into lessons. Each lesson opens with its own learning objectives so that you are clear about the skills you are focusing on. You will then be given teaching text and activities to help you learn, develop and practise those skills. Before you begin each lesson, think about how confident you are in the skills being covered. Then review your learning at the end and, if you need to, set yourself a target for further improvement.

Assessment information and practice

At the end of each unit you will be given examples of the kinds of questions and activities you will meet in the assessments. For each, you will be given guidance from the examiner on what is expected. You should have a go at completing the questions and activities. Then assess how well you have done by comparing your work to the sample answers you are given, at 'Pass' and 'Fail'. For each answer, a summary from the examiner explains what has been done well and what could be improved.

At the end of the book you will find a complete assessment practice section. Make sure you are clear about what is expected by first reading 'How you will be assessed' and 'Top Tips for success' on pages 110 to 115 before you attempt the practice papers and tasks.

ResultsPlus

These features combine expert advice and guidance from examiners to show you how to achieve better results.

Top tip
These provide guidance on how to improve your results.

ResultsPlus
Top tip

Key words in the question can help you decide which information in the text you need for your answer. Highlighting the key words in the question can help you to stay focused.

Self assessment
These help you to think about what you can do well and what needs further improvement.

ResultsPlus
Self-assessment

For each unit of work, you will be given learning objectives. Read these carefully before you start and work out how confident you feel about your skills in that area. At the end of each unit, think about how your skills have improved and what still needs further practice.

Watch out!
These warn you about common mistakes that students often make so that you can avoid them!

ResultsPlus
Watch out!

You need to use a range of reading skills to find information in a table. Scanning the layout should help you find where to look, but then you must examine the details closely to find exactly what you need.

Maximise your marks
These pages show examples of student work that is typical of what might be produced by students whose overall performance was at a Level 2 'Pass' or 'Fail'. They are taken from real students' work. The examiner has commented on the work, showing what is done well and what could be improved. The examples and comments should help you to understand what is required to achieve a Level 2 pass.

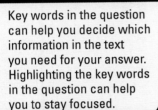

Introduction to reading

The texts and activities in this section of the book will help you to develop a range of skills for reading, understanding and comparing texts.

- You will practise using different texts to gather information, ideas, arguments, opinions and some problems.

- You will study how writers communicate meaning directly and indirectly, and consider how to respond to texts.

- At the end of the section you will find a short reading test to help you practise and assess your reading skills in the kinds of questions you will meet in the test.

- There are also sample answers at Pass and Fail, with comments from the examiner. For a full practice test, see pages 34–39.

ResultsPlus
Self-assessment

For each unit of work, you will be given learning objectives. Read these carefully before you start and work out how confident you feel about your skills in that area. At the end of each unit, think about how your skills have improved and what still needs further practice.

Your assessment

You will be assessed in one 45-minute test. You will be asked to read three texts, all about the same theme or topic, and answer questions about them. The questions will include multiple-choice and short and longer responses. For more information on how you will be assessed, see pages 110–115.

This table shows you the 'standards', or assessment objectives, that your work will be assessed against in your reading test.

Level 2 skill standard for reading: Select, read, understand and compare texts and use them to gather information, ideas, arguments and opinions.
Select and use different types of texts to obtain and utilise relevant information.
Read and summarise succinctly information/ideas from different sources.
Identify the purposes of texts and comment on how meaning is conveyed.
Detect point of view, implicit meaning and/or bias.
Analyse texts in response to audience needs and consider suitable responses.

Using text features

Your experience of reading different texts can help you to understand a new text and find information in it. Use what you know about the features of the form (for example, a letter or leaflet) to help you find information. Look out for:

▶ headings and images – these signal where different ideas are presented

▶ bold and italic fonts, capitalised words – these signal an important idea or piece of information

▶ design features that separate key chunks of text, for example boxed text and coloured panels

▶ different ways information is recorded, for example paragraphs, tables, charts or diagrams.

Activity 1

1 Study the texts below and opposite. Identify what kind of text each one is. Give **two** clues that helped you decide, for example:

> Text A is a letter. Clue 1: it begins with the greeting 'Sir...'

Text A

SIR - I have greatly appreciated the suggestions for how to chop onions without being troubled by sensitive eyes running. In particular, I tried out wearing swimming goggles but found that they steamed up. Since I could still smell the onion my eyes ran and tears filled the goggles rather than drip down my face. This made precision cutting of the onion impossible. Not only did I cut my finger but there was an uncomfortable swish of fluid around my eyes as I searched unsuccessfully for a plaster.

As the doorbell rang at that very moment for the postman to deliver a much anticipated parcel, he was somewhat bemused to see me in my dressing gown wielding a finger dripping with blood and wearing damp swimming goggles. I feel he did not quite believe my innocent explanation that I was just chopping onions.

Edward Riley

Southport

Text B

Other Parks | ThemeParks–UK
http://www.themeparks-uk.com/other-parks/

ThemeParks-UK
your guide to UK theme parks

Alton Towers   Thorpe Park   Chessington   Drayton Manor   LEGOLAND Legoland   Other Parks   A A A

SEARCH   England   Scotland   Wales

OTHER PARKS

ThemeParks-UK features comprehensive guides for five of the UK's top theme parks: Alton Towers, Thorpe Park, Chessington World of Adventures, Drayton Manor & Legoland Windsor. For each of these there are reviews and photos for the best rides, details on opening times & ticket prices, directions on how to get there, exclusive top tips, plus extra information on what's new and also what's coming in the future.

There are lots more great theme parks in the UK, this section provides a summary of the most popular.

Adventure Island
Southend-on-Sea's free admission park, where you just pay for the rides you go on. The park features roller coasters such as Green Scream and other rides for the whole family.

Camelot Theme Park
A land of great knights and amazing days, a theme park where you can see the magical sorcery of a wizard one minute and knights battling it out in spectacular jousting tournaments the next.

Activity 2

1 What does the first paragraph of Text A tell you about what the rest of the letter is going to be about?

2 Study the features of Text B. Decide where on the page you will find:
   a Which are the UK's top five theme parks.
   b Information about Adventure Island, Southend-on-Sea.
   c An overview of what the ThemeParks-UK website features.

3 Study the features of Text C on page 10. Give instructions for a reader on how to find the following information.
   a How much the line rental of the phone costs.
   b What the phone model looks like.
   c How to buy the mobile phone deal you choose.

4 Study the features of Text D on page 11.
   a What do the labels show readers?
   b Why are the words in **bold** important?
   c Why are the words in CAPITALS important?

Text C

Mobilephones.com

| Latest | Pay as you go | Reviews |

mobile phone deals

Network & Tariff	Mobile Phone Model	Average Line Rental	Minutes	Texts	Contract Deal Information
Call care 45 18 months contract	Nokia 1661 Free Phone	£9.16 regular rental £50.00	1200 minutes per month	500 text messages per month	**FREE Nokia 1661 Mobile Phone** 15 Months Reduced Line Rental of £0.99 (Usually £50.00) Redeemable Cash Back of £540.15 Redeem your cash back in five stages at month 6, 9, 12, 15 and 18 Save £735.15 on this deal Unlimited landline calls at anytime Total Contract Cost £164.85 over the 18 Months Contract Click here for more information on this deal

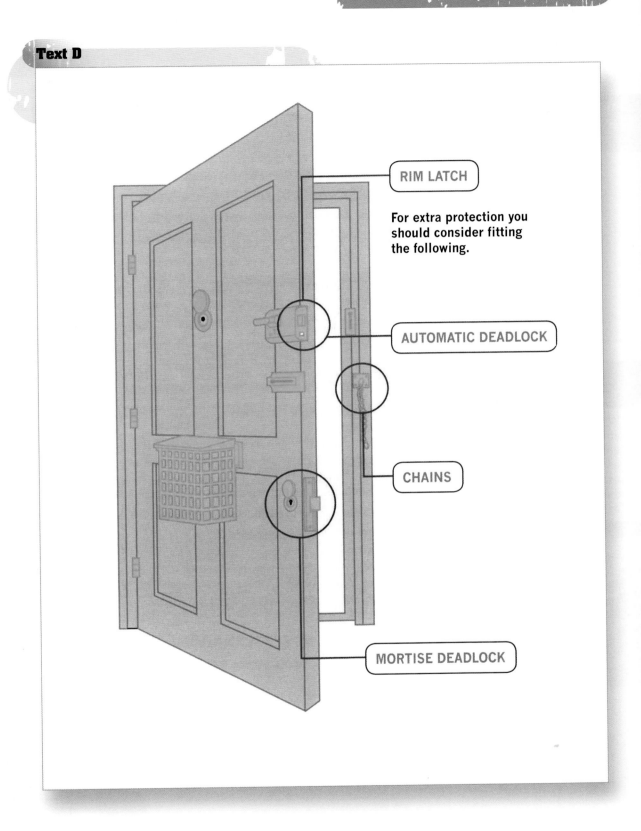

RIM LATCH

For extra protection you should consider fitting the following.

AUTOMATIC DEADLOCK

CHAINS

MORTISE DEADLOCK

This lesson will help you to:
▶ use different reading skills to find relevant information.

Skimming means looking over a text quickly to find out what it's about and what the writer is trying to do. You don't need to read every word.

Scanning means running your eyes over text features, such as headings, chunks of text and images, to find out where a particular piece of information is. You should look for **key words** rather than reading every word. A key word may be a name, number or object.

Close reading is reading carefully to get a detailed understanding. You need to read every word making sure you understand what each word and sentence means, in order to find the details you need for your answer.

You often need to use all three of these skills to find the information you need.

ResultsPlus
Top tip

When you skim the text, you might find more than one possible correct answer. If so, you must use close reading to decide which one is exactly right.

Activity 1

Use the different skills to read Text A opposite and answer the questions below.

1 **Skim** the text to find out what it is about. Which of these statements best sums it up?
   A It is a list of instructions for people wanting to live in the UK.
   B It is a list of reasons why everyone has to treat each other fairly.
   C It explains what the law says every human being's rights are.
   D It tells young people how to make the world a peaceful place.

2 **Scan** the text to find the word 'freedom' in three places, then list the three freedoms that everyone has a right to.

3 The text states that:
   A You have to be tried for a crime in secret, so that other people will not find out what you did.
   B It is ok to treat someone as guilty of a crime they are suspected of committing, before going to court, if there is evidence they did it.
   C The law is the same for everyone and we all have to be treated fairly.

   Which statement is correct?

4 Now try two of those skills together. First **scan** the text to find parts that tell you about thoughts and ideas. Then **close read** those parts and decide whether people can be forced to join a religion or political party .

Text A

TM

Universal Declaration of Human Rights
Abridged for Youth

1. We are all born free and equal. We are all born free. We all have our own thoughts and ideas. We should all be treated in the same way.

2. Don't discriminate. These rights belong to everybody, whatever our differences.

3. The right to life. We all have the right to life, and to live in freedom and safety.

4. No slavery. Nobody has any right to make us a slave. We cannot make anyone our slave.

5. No torture. Nobody has any right to hurt us or to torture us.

6. You have rights no matter where you go. I am a person just like you!

7. We're all equal before the law. The law is the same for everyone. It must treat us all fairly.

8. Your human rights are protected by law. We can all ask for the law to help us when we are not treated fairly.

9. No unfair detainment. Nobody has the right to put us in prison without good reason and keep us there, or to send us away from our country.

10. The right to trial. If we are put on trial this should be in public. The people who try us should not let anyone tell them what to do.

11. We're always innocent till proven guilty. Nobody should be blamed for doing something until it is proven. When people say we did a bad thing we have the right to show it is not true.

12. The right to privacy. Nobody should try to harm our good name. Nobody has the right to come into our home, open our letters, or bother us or our family without a good reason.

13. Freedom to move. We all have the right to go where we want in our own country and to travel as we wish.

14. The right to seek a safe place to live. If we are frightened of being badly treated in our own country, we all have the right to run away to another country to be safe.

15. Right to a nationality. We all have the right to belong to a country.

16. Marriage and family. Every grown-up has the right to marry and have a family if they want to. Men and women have the same rights when they are married, and when they are separated.

17. The right to your own things. Everyone has the right to own things or share them. Nobody should take our things from us without a good reason.

18. Freedom of thought. We all have the right to believe in what we want to believe, to have a religion, or to change it if we want.

19. Freedom of expression. We all have the right to make up our own minds, to think what we like, to say what we think, and to share our ideas with other people.

20. The right to public assembly. We all have the right to meet our friends and to work together in peace to defend our rights. Nobody can make us join a group if we don't want to.

21. The right to democracy. We all have the right to take part in the government of our country. Every grown-up should be allowed to choose their own leaders.

The **main idea** or point in a piece of text is what the text is mostly about. It is often followed by examples and **details** that add extra information to it. You need to be able to tell the difference between a main idea and a detail.

You may need to find the main point of a whole text, or of just one paragraph or section.

Paragraphs or sections will often begin with one main idea, but sometimes this does not come first. Then you have to read the whole section carefully to find out what the main idea is.

Activity 1

1 Read Text A below.

Text A

Teen Paid Surveys

Panelbase

Panelbase is fast becoming one of the most popular market research sites in the UK. For taking surveys here you will be rewarded with between 50p and £10 which is added straight into your Panelbase account. As soon as you reach £10 you can redeem your balance for either a cash payment sent straight to your bank account, a cheque or various high street gift vouchers. Each online survey you are sent takes on average around 15 minutes to complete. As soon as you have registered with Panelbase £3 will be instantly added into your account. Teenagers aged 16 and over are welcome to join.

Survey Pays: 50p – £10
Age: 16+
Reward: Cash (Earn £3 instantly for registering)

2 Which of these statements best sums up the text's main point?
  A The surveys are done online.
  B Panelbase pays people money or gift vouchers for taking surveys.
  C It will take around 15 minutes to complete one survey.
  D Panelbase is a market research company rewarding teenagers for taking surveys.

3 Which of the above statements are about a detail rather than the main focus?

1 Read Text B below.

 ### Teen Paid Surveys

Paid Surveys for Teens - Get paid to be young!

 Easy teenage job. Want an online part time job to do in your spare time?

Want to earn lots of extra cash and be given the chance to win hundreds of prizes?

Now is your big chance – market-research companies need teenage opinions to help influence what new products and services are introduced in the future. Survey topics include everything from the latest Movies, Fashion, Jewellery, PC and Console games, Sports, Electronics, Shopping and much more.

For sharing your opinion and completing online surveys you will be rewarded with cash, high street vouchers, free CDs, cinema tickets, online music downloads, the chance to win thousands of prizes and much much more... This has to be the easiest online job for teenagers!

Teen Paid Surveys will only ever list market-research companies that are free to join. For each and every market research site Teen Paid Surveys provides you with full descriptions, what reward you will get for completing the surveys and what age you have to be to join.

Our aim is to provide teens with a safe, free and fun way to earn extra money and get rewarded online for completing paid surveys, the perfect teen job.

Go to our hints and tips section to read our frequently asked questions on completing teen paid surveys.

If you want to be sent loads of surveys every month then sign up to all the sites listed below and earn loads of extra cash!!

Remember, once you've registered, to completely fill in your profile on each of the various sites. This will make sure that you get as many paid surveys as possible.

Remember to use your own words when answering the questions below.

2 According to the text, why do market research companies want teenage opinions?

3 According to the text which three things do the Teen Paid Surveys service offer teenagers who take part?

4 What is the main idea of the text?

 Results**Plus**
Top tip

'According to the text' means you should only use information in the relevant text. You will get no marks for other information or ideas.

Comparing texts

This lesson will help you to:
▶ compare two texts
▶ choose and use different texts to find relevant information.

Comparing two different texts means searching to find:

▶ ways they are the **same**

▶ how they are **different**.

Step 1 Start by reading through the first text carefully, picking out its main ideas and points.

Step 2 Begin to read the second text. Keep asking yourself: 'Does it say something similar to what was in the other text?' 'In what ways is this different from the other text?'

Step 3 Go back to the first text and search it to find out whether it says something similar to or different from what you have just read.

Step 4 If there are more texts, go through the steps.

Activity 1

1 Read Text A. Which of these statements are true?
   A There is only one way to score a goal in football.
   B The 'away goals' rule applies to every away match.
   C A team loses a game of football even if they score a draw.

2 Read Text B. Which of these statements are false?
   A There are three ways to score a point.
   B A player scoring a try will get fewer points than by scoring a dropped goal and making a conversion.
   C A player must have his hand on the ball before it crosses the goal line.

3 Now consider the two texts.
   a In what ways are football and rugby **as described in Texts A and B** similar?
   b In what ways are football and rugby **as described in Texts A and B** different?

ResultsPlus
Watch out!

Read the questions carefully. You could lose marks if you do not understand fully what you are being asked to do. If you are asked to make three points make sure you do.

Text A

Howdy! **Login - Signup**

Talkfootball.co.uk | Home | Blog | Forum | **Guide** | Search Talk Football | Talkon.it

Talk Football » The Guide » The Rules of Football

My Account

Login or Signup for a free Talk Football account!

Talk Football Guide

Rules ↓

Golden Goal

Penalty Kicks

Scoring

A team can only score, if the whole ball crosses the goal line between the goalposts. The winner is the team who scores more goals, except in a competition where the 'away goals' rule applies. The 'away goals' rule means that, if a team scores a goal away from their home stadium, the goal counts for more (therefore, a 1-1 scoreline would mean the away team wins).

Text B

Scoring in Rugby

Players must score a **try** or a **goal** to win points.

A try

A try is worth 5 points. To score a try, a player has to take the ball across the goal line and then place it on the ground with their hand still on it. This is called grounding.

A goal

To score a goal a player has to kick the ball between the upright posts and above the crossbar of the goal posts. There are three types of goal.

1 A dropped goal, worth 3 points – this is scored during normal play. The ball must hit the ground and immediately be kicked over the crossbar.

2 A penalty goal, worth 3 points – a team is awarded the chance to try for a penalty goal when the opposing side has infringed a rugby rule. The ball can be stationary on the ground and kicked (place kick), or dropped and kicked (drop kick).

3 A conversion, worth 2 points – this is awarded after a try is scored. A drop kick or stationary kick can be used.

5 Selecting relevant information from more than one text

To select relevant information from texts, follow these steps:

1 Decide what you need to find out.

2 Choose texts that look as if they contain the right kind of information.

3 Search those texts, scanning them for key words and phrases.

4 Work out whether the information you have found is relevant.

After reading a section of text, ask yourself: 'Does it tell me what I needed to know?'

The extracts from the website and the report in Texts A, B and C opposite tell readers about the work of the Jamie Oliver Foundation and the restaurant Fifteen.

Activity 1

1 Decide which of the three texts opposite you need to read to find out:
  a Some of the costs of helping a chef apprentice.
  b What kind of people are taken on to the training scheme.
  c What Jamie Oliver thinks the Foundation offers young people.

2 a Read the profiles of the two people below. They are both are thinking of applying to go on the training course.

Ash is 19, homeless and unemployed. Mostly he eats tinned food and microwave ready-meals. He hasn't held down a job since he left school at 15. Ash did not attend school regularly. He is looking for a fresh start.

Emily is an unemployed single mum, aged 23. She lives in London and loves cooking, although she doesn't think she's very good at it. She wants to build a better life for her baby and herself.

  b Consider the information about Ash and Emily, and the criteria given in Text C. Based on this information, is Ash or Emily most qualified to become an apprentice? Why?

Text A

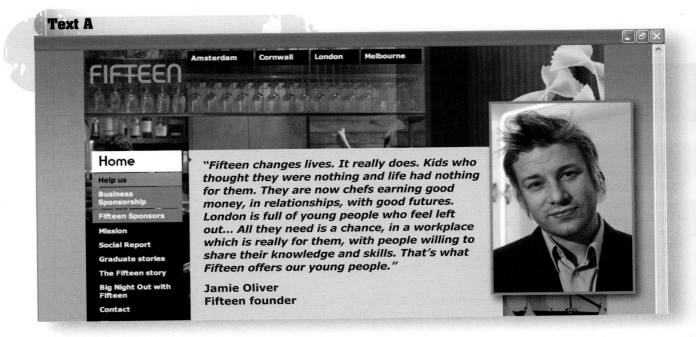

Amsterdam · Cornwall · London · Melbourne

FIFTEEN

Home

Help us

Business Sponsorship

Fifteen Sponsors

Mission

Social Report

Graduate stories

The Fifteen story

Big Night Out with Fifteen

Contact

"Fifteen changes lives. It really does. Kids who thought they were nothing and life had nothing for them. They are now chefs earning good money, in relationships, with good futures. London is full of young people who feel left out... All they need is a chance, in a workplace which is really for them, with people willing to share their knowledge and skills. That's what Fifteen offers our young people."

Jamie Oliver
Fifteen founder

Text B

It costs money to change lives – no matter how thin or bulky your wallet you can make a difference.

Here are a few examples of what it costs to develop each apprentice into a fantastic chef:

Chef's knives & whites	£50
Weekly travel costs	£35
Weekly living allowance	£40
Work placements	£100
Selection of apprentices	£170
Housing support	£200
Training trips	£350

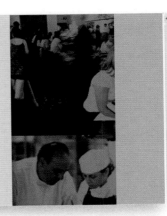

Text C

The criteria

- 18 to 24 years of age
- Not in education, employment or training
- Living in Greater London
- Able to work in the UK
- Able to commit to a year

Plus we look for

- Passion for food
- A genuine desire to be a chef
- Someone up for the challenge and a fresh start

This lesson will help you to:
► use tables to find relevant information.

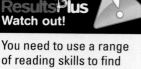
Watch out!

You need to use a range of reading skills to find information in a table. Scanning the layout should help you find where to look, but then you must examine the details closely to find exactly what you need.

Follow these instructions to find numbers, words or symbols in a table:

1 Read the heading of each row and column.

2 Scan the table for symbols, words and numbers. Make sure you understand what all parts of the table mean by reading the key.

3 Decide what you need to find out. Scan to find the right row or column to look at.

4 Move your finger along and keep **scanning** until you find the information. Then close read that part of the text to find the details you need.

Activity 1

Josh is planning a trip to Manchester city centre. He wants to stay in a hotel no further than 0.6 miles from the centre. He is looking for a hotel rated four stars or above. Read the chart showing available hotels on the opposite page, and answer the questions below.

1 Which hotels on the list are close enough to the city centre for Josh?

2 Which of the hotels best match what Josh requires?

3 Josh also decides he wants to spend a maximum of £75 per night. Which of the hotels from his shortlist should he choose?

4 If you wanted to stay in a hotel with the highest guest rating, which of these should you choose?
  A The Abode
  B The Lowry A Rocco Forte Hotel
  C Velvet Hotel
  D Ramada Manchester Piccadilly

5 How far are the two five-star hotels from Manchester city centre?

6 How far in miles from Manchester city centre is the least expensive hotel on 8 January?
  A 0.1
  B 0.6
  C 2.9
  D 3.5

7 You wish to stay at a four-star hotel with a special offer. List two hotels which you could view?

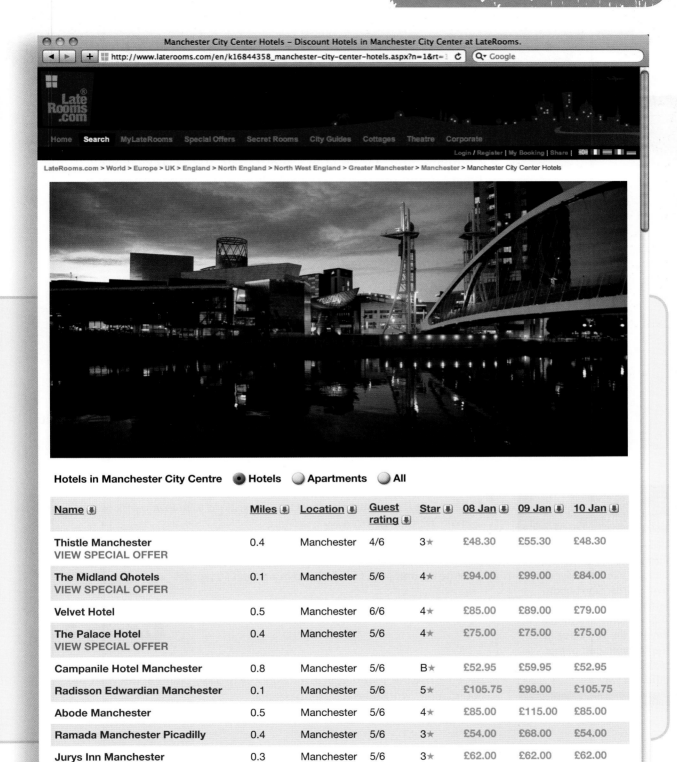

Manchester City Center Hotels – Discount Hotels in Manchester City Center at LateRooms.

http://www.laterooms.com/en/k16844358_manchester-city-center-hotels.aspx?n=1&rt=1

Q Google

Late Rooms .com

Home · **Search** · MyLateRooms · Special Offers · Secret Rooms · City Guides · Cottages · Theatre · Corporate

Login / Register | My Booking | Share |

LateRooms.com > World > Europe > UK > England > North England > North West England > Greater Manchester > Manchester > Manchester City Center Hotels

Hotels in Manchester City Centre   ● Hotels   ○ Apartments   ○ All

Name ⬇	Miles ⬇	Location ⬇	Guest rating ⬇	Star ⬇	08 Jan ⬇	09 Jan ⬇	10 Jan ⬇
Thistle Manchester VIEW SPECIAL OFFER	0.4	Manchester	4/6	3★	£48.30	£55.30	£48.30
The Midland Qhotels VIEW SPECIAL OFFER	0.1	Manchester	5/6	4★	£94.00	£99.00	£84.00
Velvet Hotel	0.5	Manchester	6/6	4★	£85.00	£89.00	£79.00
The Palace Hotel VIEW SPECIAL OFFER	0.4	Manchester	5/6	4★	£75.00	£75.00	£75.00
Campanile Hotel Manchester	0.8	Manchester	5/6	B★	£52.95	£59.95	£52.95
Radisson Edwardian Manchester	0.1	Manchester	5/6	5★	£105.75	£98.00	£105.75
Abode Manchester	0.5	Manchester	5/6	4★	£85.00	£115.00	£85.00
Ramada Manchester Picadilly	0.4	Manchester	5/6	3★	£54.00	£68.00	£54.00
Jurys Inn Manchester	0.3	Manchester	5/6	3★	£62.00	£62.00	£62.00
The Lowry A Rocco Forte Hotel	0.4	Manchester	5/6	5★	£119.00	£149.00	£119.00
Days Hotel Manchester City VIEW SPECIAL OFFER	0.6	Manchester	5/6	3★	£35.00	£60.00	£35.00
Best Western Princess on Portland A Folio Hotel	0.3	Manchester	5/6	3★	£59.00	£89.00	£69.00

Summarising means writing a short account of the main points. To write a summary, follow these steps:

1 Search different texts to find relevant information.

2 Compare information found in different places. Ask yourself: 'What have I found out in each place? What is the same and what is different?'

3 Summarise the information. To do this:

▶ include only relevant and essential information

▶ don't repeat things

▶ if there are lists of information, sum up what they are about. For example, sum up a list telling you the different achievements of famous footballers as: 'lots of famous footballers' achievements' instead of listing each one separately

▶ find each paragraph's main point (or main idea) to help you sum it up

▶ pick out and use key words and phrases

▶ keep trimming and improving your summary until you are sure it is as tight as possible and includes all the key points.

ResultsPlus
Watch out!

When summarising information from a text you need to use mostly your own words. Don't quote large chunks from the text. A good summary should include the key ideas in the relevant part of the text expressed in a slightly different way.

Activity 1

1 Read Text A opposite. Then use these questions to help you pick out the main information from each section:

Who? **What?** **When?** **Where?** **How?** **Why?**

2 Write a summary of Text A in no more than 50 words.

Activity 2

Study Text A about the Jamie Oliver Foundation and the restaurant Fifteen on page 19. Use the information in it to identify two key points about what the Foundation's work does for young people.

Text A

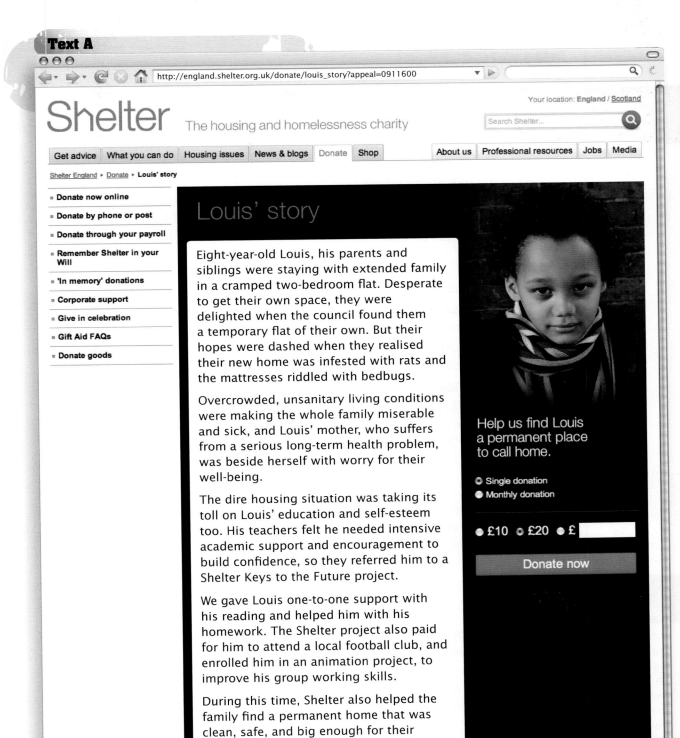

http://england.shelter.org.uk/donate/louis_story?appeal=0911600

Search Shelter...

Your location: **England** / Scotland

Shelter

The housing and homelessness charity

Get advice | What you can do | Housing issues | News & blogs | Donate | Shop | About us | Professional resources | Jobs | Media

Shelter England ▸ Donate ▸ Louis' story

- **Donate now online**
- **Donate by phone or post**
- **Donate through your payroll**
- **Remember Shelter in your Will**
- **'In memory' donations**
- **Corporate support**
- **Give in celebration**
- **Gift Aid FAQs**
- **Donate goods**

Louis' story

Eight-year-old Louis, his parents and siblings were staying with extended family in a cramped two-bedroom flat. Desperate to get their own space, they were delighted when the council found them a temporary flat of their own. But their hopes were dashed when they realised their new home was infested with rats and the mattresses riddled with bedbugs.

Overcrowded, unsanitary living conditions were making the whole family miserable and sick, and Louis' mother, who suffers from a serious long-term health problem, was beside herself with worry for their well-being.

The dire housing situation was taking its toll on Louis' education and self-esteem too. His teachers felt he needed intensive academic support and encouragement to build confidence, so they referred him to a Shelter Keys to the Future project.

We gave Louis one-to-one support with his reading and helped him with his homework. The Shelter project also paid for him to attend a local football club, and enrolled him in an animation project, to improve his group working skills.

During this time, Shelter also helped the family find a permanent home that was clean, safe, and big enough for their needs. Louis' schoolwork and confidence are vastly improved, and the family now feel they can finally put down roots, and begin afresh.

Help us find Louis a permanent place to call home.

○ Single donation
● Monthly donation

● £10 ○ £20 ● £ [   ]

Donate now

8 Understanding the purpose of a text

To understand a text's purpose fully you will need to work out what sort of text it is, what the writer hopes to achieve and who it is meant to be read by. For example, to give advice to teenage website readers about how to meet a celebrity. To decide on a text's purpose, work through these steps:

1 **Look at the whole text** and the way it is laid out. What kind of text do you think it is? Check if you are right by searching for the kinds of features that you expect that type of text to have. For example, a webpage might have headings, images, links, menus and short chunks of text. If you can't find what you are expecting, you may need to think again.

2 **Read the text** and ask yourself:
   ▶ 'What does the writer want the reader to do?'
     For example, to follow the writer's advice.
   ▶ 'What does the writer want to do for the reader?'
     For example, to give advice to the reader.

3 **Decide who the text has been written for.** The kinds of words used and the way the writer addresses the reader should help you to work it out. For example, some kinds of slang words or casual speech might show it is aimed at teenagers.

Activity 1

1 Study Text A opposite. Following the steps listed above, work out what its purpose is and write this out as a sentence.

2 What is the main purpose of Text B, opposite?

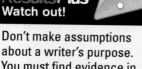
ResultsPlus
Watch out!

Don't make assumptions about a writer's purpose. You must find evidence in the text to support your ideas, for example, in the way information and ideas are presented.

Activity 2

1 With a partner, study the texts on page 9–11. Decide on the purpose of each text and write it down.

2 Work with another pair and compare your summaries. Do you agree? If not, discuss why you disagree and then work together to write a sentence you can all agree on.

Text A

Five simple steps to sunshine safe skin

1. Wear loose-fitting clothing and a wide-brimmed hat when in the sun.
2. Apply sunscreen 15–30 minutes before going out in the sun and reapply every couple of hours throughout the day. Remember to reapply when you emerge from cooling off in the water and never use sunscreen to extend the time you would normally spend in the sun.
3. Seek out shade, particularly between 11am and 3pm, when the sun is usually at its most intense.
4. Be aware of the danger to your skin when choosing to apply a temporary tattoo on holiday. A temporary tattoo may illegally contain PPD. As a simple rule, if it is called 'black henna' or it is black or dark, don't do it! It can cause reactions in your skin and affect your skin's health in the long run.
5. Drink plenty of water, particularly in hot weather. Keeping your water intake high prevents dehydration and maintains healthy kidneys and bladder, and a healthy body helps to support healthy skin.

Text B

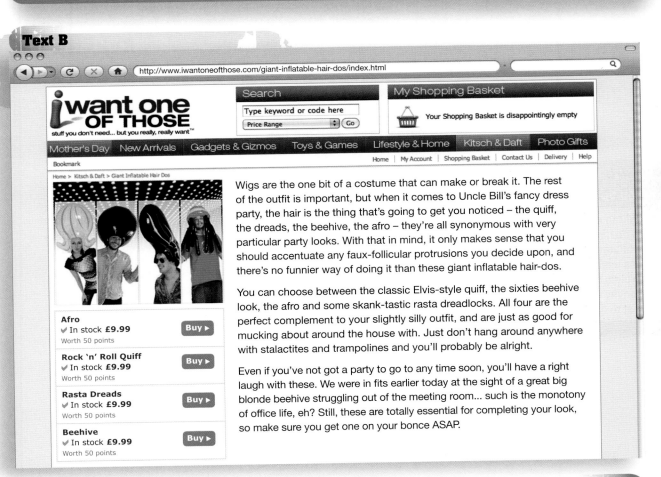

http://www.iwantoneofthose.com/giant-inflatable-hair-dos/index.html

i want one OF THOSE
stuff you don't need... but you really, really want™

Search
Type keyword or code here
Price Range | Go

My Shopping Basket
Your Shopping Basket is disappointingly empty

Mother's Day | New Arrivals | Gadgets & Gizmos | Toys & Games | Lifestyle & Home | Kitsch & Daft | Photo Gifts

Home | My Account | Shopping Basket | Contact Us | Delivery | Help

Bookmark

Home > Kitsch & Daft > Giant Inflatable Hair Dos

Afro
✔ In stock **£9.99**
Worth 50 points
[Buy ▶]

Rock 'n' Roll Quiff
✔ In stock **£9.99**
Worth 50 points
[Buy ▶]

Rasta Dreads
✔ In stock **£9.99**
Worth 50 points
[Buy ▶]

Beehive
✔ In stock **£9.99**
Worth 50 points
[Buy ▶]

Wigs are the one bit of a costume that can make or break it. The rest of the outfit is important, but when it comes to Uncle Bill's fancy dress party, the hair is the thing that's going to get you noticed – the quiff, the dreads, the beehive, the afro – they're all synonymous with very particular party looks. With that in mind, it only makes sense that you should accentuate any faux-follicular protrusions you decide upon, and there's no funnier way of doing it than these giant inflatable hair-dos.

You can choose between the classic Elvis-style quiff, the sixties beehive look, the afro and some skank-tastic rasta dreadlocks. All four are the perfect complement to your slightly silly outfit, and are just as good for mucking about around the house with. Just don't hang around anywhere with stalactites and trampolines and you'll probably be alright.

Even if you've not got a party to go to any time soon, you'll have a right laugh with these. We were in fits earlier today at the sight of a great big blonde beehive struggling out of the meeting room... such is the monotony of office life, eh? Still, these are totally essential for completing your look, so make sure you get one on your bonce ASAP.

9 How writers communicate meaning

Writers express meaning through the points they make and the way they make them. Work through these three steps to help you to decide how meaning is communicated in texts:

1 What is the purpose of the text? Pinpoint how you can tell, for example, if it says 'Buy now!'

2 How is the text written? Look at:

▶ How it is organised on the page – what headings, bullet lists, images, diagrams etc. are used to help readers find information.

▶ What it tells readers – what facts, opinions, evidence, advice etc. are included. Does it tell the readers everything they need to know? For example, an advert might give facts about the product and opinions such as 'excellent value'.

▶ The words and phrases the writer uses. Do they suit the audience and situation – for example, are they too informal?

3 How does the way the text is written help the text achieve its purpose? For example, using persuasive words like 'luxury that is affordable' appeals to readers because they want to treat themselves, but don't want to get into debt.

Activity 1

1 Read Text A opposite and note down what its purpose is.

2 a Which of the features below are used in the text opposite?

**heading   caption   bullet points   list   image
paragraphs   pull-out box**

b What does each one tell the reader?

3 In your own words, explain what each paragraph tells the reader.

4 Do the words and phrases in the text suit its purpose, audience and situation? Pick out three examples and use them to prove that your point of view is sensible. For example, 'The writer uses words that keen cyclists would know, such as…'

5 a How effectively has the writer communicated his meaning to readers in this text?

b Suggest one way in which the writer could improve the text so that it achieves its purpose better.

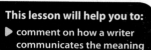

Results Plus
Top tip

For top marks, you need to do more than just say what techniques the writer has used. You must also explain how they help to convey the meaning of the text to the reader.

Text A

THE RYEDALE RUMBLE – SUNDAY, AUGUST 9

Get ready to Rumble: ride the North York Moors

If you haven't ridden in the North York Moors before then you really don't know what you're missing.

This year's event will see the start date pushed back to August 9. According to organiser Bob Howden, 'You only have to see the North York Moors in August and the reason hits you straight away. The hills are a carpet of purple heather that take your breath away if the climbs haven't already!'

117 MILES LONG

The 2009 edition is a repeat of the route introduced last year. Starting at the splendid Gilling Castle, and the home of St Martin's Ampleforth School, the riders depart on any of three rides of 116.9 miles (Rumble 1), 83.8 miles (Rumble 2) and 55.6 miles (Rumble 3).

Timing certificates are available and you can celebrate with your post-event meal in the splendour of the castle's panelled dining hall, reliving experiences of one of the toughest 'must do' sportives. For further details go to www.ryedalerumble.co.uk.

Activity 2

1 Work as a group. Choose any feature text in this book. Think together how you could improve the text you have chosen, to make it easier for readers to find and compare the information in it. Make a list of suggested changes.

10 Understanding implied meanings

This lesson will help you to:
▶ understand meanings that are hinted at or suggested.
▶ be able to identify facts and opinions.

Sometimes writers say things in a straightforward way, for example, 'Go to Malaysia on holiday', but they may also imply other meanings. This means that they hint at or suggest things in their writing.

For example, look at this extract from a tourism website:

> Malaysia has superb golden beaches, lush vegetation, mountains and fabulous shopping <u>allied to some magnificent hotels</u>.

What are the underlined words hinting at? Perhaps it is a hint that there are no quality shops away from the hotels?

Writers may use facts and opinions in their writing. It is important to be able to identify these, as writers may present their opinions as if they were facts to support their point of view.

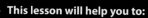

ResultsPlus
Watch out!

Be on the lookout for ideas and opinions which are suggested indirectly through the language or layout of the text. Ask yourself – is this a fact, or just the writer's opinion?

Activity 1

1 Which sentences in Text A opposite hint at or suggest these ideas?
   a The letter is written by Santa Claus.
   b Santa Claus thinks that over the years people have become greedy.
   c The gifts on offer at Carphone Warehouse are very sophisticated.

2 Which of the following statements **best** sums up which implied meaning is being suggested to readers. How?
   A Carphone Warehouse want readers to visit them.
   B Carphone Warehouse want readers to think their products are sophisticated.
   C Carphone Warehouse think it is time Santa Claus retired and they took over.

Read the Text B on the page opposite. Decide whether each of the following statements about the cottage taken from it are Fact or Opinion.

Activity 2

Statement	Fact	Opinion
A ... a superb holiday home.		
B It is situated just 700 metres above the coastal road.		
C ... has an open plan, fully fitted kitchen, spacious lounge, master bedroom with king sized bed and en suite.		
D ... superb views... beautiful turquoise waters.		
E ... The patio doors in the master bedroom lead on to a balcony.		

Text A

Dear Talik

After centuries of reading the world's begging letters, trespassing on private property, stuffing stockings and eating stale mince pies – I give up! There was a time when folks would make do with a satsuma and a pair of newly darned socks. But these days it's all flashing gizmos and shoot 'em ups. How can I compete, eh? It's just me, a sleigh, eight tired reindeer and some sizzled elves.

And now this: the Carphone Warehouse Christmas brochure. It's packed with the latest technology and loads of great gifts. Apparently, all this stuff has been 'specially' handpicked for Christmas. Oooh lardy-dah! And we're not talking some inflatable sheep and Hello Kitty earmuffs, oh no! We're talking cutting edge laptops and stylish touchscreen phones – as well as FREE Nintendo Wiis and PS3 Lites with selected deals. They say this is the sort of fancy pants gear so-called hipsters go gaga for.

If that's not enough, they've also got great deals on home and mobile broadband. And guess what? Some of these deals even come with FREE laptops! Pah!

But don't just take my word for it. After all, I'm nothing more than a pin-up for fizzy drinks commercials. See for yourself what The Carphone Warehouse has to offer.

Yours flying to Bermuda,

Santa Claus

Text B

A superb holiday home with private pool and wonderful panoramic views. Crocus Cottage is near the picturesque village of St Brede's Cornwall. It is situated just 700 meters above the coastal road so St Brede's is within easy reach of the upmarket village of Carlton.

This comfortable cottage has an open plan, fully-fitted kitchen, spacious lounge, master bedroom with king-size bed and en suite. There are two further twin bedded rooms both with en suite bathroom/shower rooms. The patio doors in the master bedroom lead on to a balcony with table and seating, and provide superb views stretching across the countryside to the beautiful turquoise waters of the sea.

This lesson will help you to:

▶ recognise points of view and bias

▶ understand how these can affect meaning.

Someone's point of view includes their opinions, thoughts and feelings about a topic. Writers may back up their ideas using facts, arguments and evidence. A balanced view of a topic, includes different points of view. A writer who only gives one side of the argument is showing bias.

You can work out a writer's point of view by finding words that reveal their feelings ('I feel', 'I love', 'it's terrible', 'it's wonderful'); beliefs ('should', 'ought', 'must', 'need to'); thoughts ('I think', 'in my opinion', 'I agree with', 'most people think').

Top tip

Look closely at the words the writer has chosen which may give clues about their point of view and bias. In questions where you are asked to respond in writing, give examples from the text to support your answer.

Activity 1

1 Read Text A below.

  a Pick out words and phrases that reveal Jo Swinson's point of view.

  b Which of these statements best sums up the Liberal Democrats' point of view?

    A Airbrushing is a form of lying so it is wrong.

    B Airbrushed images put pressure on young people who think that is how they should look.

    C Companies should be free to advertise in the best way to sell their product.

Text A

http://www.telegraph.co.uk/news/newstopics/politics/

Airbrushing of photos should be banned, Liberal Democrats say

Magazines should be banned from airbrushing photographs in adverts aimed at young people, the Liberal Democrats say

By Rosa Prince, Political Correspondent

As part of a new policy on women's issues, the party suggests all images should be accompanied by a message indicating if they have been airbrushed – the term used when photographs are doctored to make the subject look thinner or free of blemishes.

Jo Swinson, the MP for East Dunbartonshire, said: 'Today's unrealistic idea of what is beautiful means that young girls are under more pressure now than they were even five years ago.

'Airbrushing mean that adverts contain completely unattainable images that no one can live up to in real life.

'We need to help protect children from these pressures and we need to make a start by banning airbrushing in adverts aimed at them.

'Liberal Democrats believe in the freedom of companies to advertise but we also believe in the freedom of young people to develop their self-esteem and to be as comfortable as possible with their bodies, without constantly feeling the need to measure up to a very narrow range of digitally manipulated shapes and sizes.'

The party will call on the Advertising Standards Authority to ban all altered or enhanced images in advertising aimed at the under-16s.

Activity 2

1 Read Text B.
   a Pick out the words and phrases that reveal the writer's point of view.
   b What evidence does the writer give to back up this point of view?

Text B

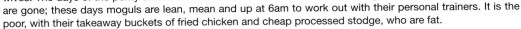

Lighten up – Kate Moss is right

Eleanor Mills, Timesonline

'Nothing tastes as good as skinny feels,' Kate Moss trilled last week. Her little motto has been damned as the phrase that will launch a thousand eating disorders.

Is that really fair? Most women would – broadly – agree with Moss. At the moment I'm rather pleased that I can get into jeans that haven't fitted for years. It feels good. I am 38 and I've had two children; if I am not going to become a large lump, I have to work out and keep off the croissants. I have the odd one – life's for living. I don't want to be 'skinny'; just fit and healthy. But in our sedentary times it requires effort to avoid being lardy; that's why nearly a quarter of Britons are obese (that's a body mass index of 30-plus, not just a muffin top).

In the 21st century, thin equals success: posh clothes shops don't make big sizes; rich footballers marry skinny birds. And fat is no longer just a feminine issue. These days men, worried about the moobs, are every bit as likely to refuse the bread at lunch as their wives. The days of the porky chief executive with his 'chauffeur chub' and long lunches are gone; these days moguls are lean, mean and up at 6am to work out with their personal trainers. It is the poor, with their takeaway buckets of fried chicken and cheap processed stodge, who are fat.

So Moss is not wrong to say that you feel better if you are slim. The problem is, she is the most powerful woman in British fashion, and it is that industry, with its retouched images of unreal perfection, that is blamed for the eating disorders that ruin the lives of so many young women. The problem with Moss saying, 'Nothing tastes as good as skinny feels,' is that our culture has a very sick underbelly that takes her literally.

Activity 3

1 a Think about both the texts you have just read. Which text presents a balanced point of view and which has bias?
   b Give two reasons why the text you have chosen might be biased.

2 Now read Text C below. Consider to whom the text has been written for and if the text is biased. For example, does the writer assume that the reader shares their opinion?

Text C

Now in fashion ...

DENIM SHIRTS!

A key look for this season is layering. "Teen Mag's" fashion experts are saying that denim shirts go with anything from skinny jeans, leggings and T-shirts, to skirts and dresses. Loads of celebs are wearing vintage denim shirts, layered with other season's trends. Denim shirts are all about this year's key trend: the 1980s! Wearing a vintage denim shirt makes it look like you've just thrown on your bloke's shirt. Who would have known our boyfriends had such desirable wardrobes!

12 Consider suitable responses to texts

A text is written to suit an audience and to achieve a purpose. The reader needs to decide whether to respond to the text in the way the writer wants. For example, a text's purpose might be to offer advice – the reader has to decide if they would be wise to act on that advice.

Use these questions to help you problem solve and decide how to respond to a text:

▶ What is the text's intended purpose?
▶ Who is the text's intended audience?
▶ Does the writer give all the information you need to decide how to respond?
▶ Does the writer use words and phrases that suit the audience and situation?
▶ Does the text seem trustworthy and the information in it reliable?
▶ What is a sensible response to the text?

Activity 1

1 Read Text A below.
   a What is the text's purpose?
   b Who is the text's audience?
   c Does the advice tell readers what they need to know?
   d Does the writer use language that is appropriate to the audience and situation?
   d Pick out three words or phrases that show the writer understands how scams work.
   e Would it be appropriate to give this leaflet to someone who was worried they might be the victim of a scam? Why?

Text A

How scam artists succeed

They will:

● catch you unawares, contacting you without you asking them to, by phone, email, post or sometimes in person
● sound pleasant, well-spoken and kind (on the phone or at your door) and want you to think they are your friend
● have slick and professional leaflets and letters
● be persistent and persuasive
● rush you into making a decision
● ask you to send money before you receive their tempting offer or win a prize.

New scams from the UK and overseas appear every day – **so it's important to know how to spot them.**

Activity 2

1 a What is the purpose of Text B?
  b List the features that you would you expect a business letter from a consultant for an international company to have. Does this letter contain these features?
  c Consider the information given in Texts A and B. Should the reader respond to this letter and apply for the job? Give reasons for your answer.

Text B

Alldays Co Ltd.
Limpopo
South Africa

Hello

Pleasant day, I have good news about a job offer you might be interested in. My name is smith Pearson, i am 39 of age and i work for Alldays Co Ltd as a consultant. We extract raw materials from Africa to produce textiles and fabrics which we supply to our international clients. We are looking for part time employee based in different parts of the world and our focus very much on North American and Europe. We are willing to pay 6 dollars US for every transaction which wouldn't affect your present state of work. My company is based in South Africa and we need someone who is responsible and reliable and would help us receive payments from our customers until we have set up our branches all over ever ywhere if it is possible. All you have to do is help us receive payments from our customers in your country or in a neighbouring country. These payments are in checks and they would come to you in your name and all you need to do is cash it, deduct your commission and send the rest to us using western union. But sometimes the police get involved in case someone tries to run off our money, i hope it is ok and you are interested i would send you an employment letter which you are to sign and send back to me as soon as possible and i would need you to give me your full name, address, email, and your phone number for me to get in contact with you,

Best regards
Smith Pearson

Read Text A and answer the questions which follow.

Address http://www.citizencard.com/faq.php   Go   Links »

CITiZENCARD

Go to

NEWS | ABOUT US | FAQ | RETAILERS | RETAILER CO-BRANDS | CARD UPTAKE | CONTACT US

APPLY
FOR A CITIZENCARD
CLICK HERE ▶▶

▸ Why do I need a CitizenCard?

Many organisations need to be sure of your age or identity. Using a CitizenCard is voluntary, but it can make life much easier. Even if you have a passport or driving licence, CitizenCard means you can leave these more valuable documents safely at home. Using a CitizenCard means that you can access the products and services to which you are entitled.

▸ Is CitizenCard widely recognised?

Most shops, pubs, clubs, airlines (domestic flights) and other organisations recognise CitizenCard as valid photo-ID or proof-of-age. CitizenCard was the first scheme to carry PASS (Proof of Age Standards Scheme) accreditation, supported by the Home Office.

▸ Can anyone apply ?

Babies, children, adults – anyone can now obtain a CitizenCard. If you are under 16 you will need parental consent.

▸ How do I apply for a card ?

You can download an application form or collect one from most supermarkets, convenience stores, off licences, post offices or newsagents. Complete the form and send it to CitizenCard with your payment.

▸ What exactly do I need to send with my application form?

To avoid any unnecessary delays in producing your card, please ensure you have fully completed the application form. Please enclose:

1 Two photos, one of which must be signed by an eligible verifier. A verifier must be at least 25 years old and be in a recognised profession. They must not be a relative or be in a personal relationship with you nor live at the same address.

2 A photocopy of your birth certificate or certified copy of birth certificate, passport, photo-driving licence, NHS medical card, National Insurance card or National Identity Card which must be signed by an eligible verifier. Please DO NOT send original documents.

3 Your payment.

▸ How much does a CitizenCard cost (UK)? How do I pay?

Using the online application form, the standard cost is £15. Urgent applications cost £30.

Payment must be made by credit/debit card or postal order. If you send a postal order please make it payable to **Citizencard Limited.** Please do not send cash.

1 What is the **main** purpose of Text A?

(1 mark)

Answer Question 2 with a cross in the box (☒). If you change your mind about an answer, put a line through the box (☒) and then mark your new answer with a cross (☒).

2 Anyone signing documents to verify your identity must be:

☐	A	living at the same address
☐	B	working in any job
☐	C	25 years old or over
☐	D	closely related to you

(1 mark)

3 Identify **two** reasons for buying a CitizenCard, according to Text A.

You do not need to write in sentences.

i) ....

....

ii) ....

....

(2 marks)

Read Text B and answer the questions which follow.

Text B

http://nds.coi.gov.uk/content/detail.aspx?NewsAreaId=2&ReleaseID=410552&SubjectId=2

News Distribution Service
for Government and the Public Sector

COI

Young people in London to get National Identity Cards

Young people aged 16 to 24 who live in London will be able to apply for a National Identity Card from 8 February, it was announced today.

The rollout to young people in the capital follows the successful uptake of cards in Greater Manchester and the North West of England.

The £30 identity card provides a secure and convenient way for people to prove their identity whether they are travelling in Europe – the cards can also be used in place of a passport for travel throughout Europe – or buying age-restricted goods.

Young people across the capital buying alcohol, computer games and DVDs, going to the cinema or to a club, know how important it is to have a recognised proof of identity which is easy to carry.

Research by the Identity and Passport Service shows that over half of lost and stolen passports belong to people under 30, and a tenth of those are lost by people using them as ID on a night out. As an ID card fits snugly into a wallet, it should help avoid the card becoming lost.

Also, until 30 June, people across the UK who have registered an interest through the Directgov website will be able to apply for a card. More than 16,000 people have already registered an interest in getting an identity card in this way.

Meg Hillier, the Home Office Minister responsible for identity cards said:

"The National Identity Card will prove an extremely useful tool for young people in London, whether they are opening a bank account, buying age-restricted goods such as computer games or DVDs, entering a nightclub or travelling to Europe.

"These benefits are already being enjoyed by members of the public in Greater Manchester and the North West of England and with tough new legislation being put in place clamping down on underage drinking, it will be more important than ever for young people to have access to a universally accepted proof of age."

Suleman Khonat, President of the National Federation of Retail Newsagents, said:

"Independent newsagents and convenience store owners are pleased that the introduction of national identity cards is to be rolled out to London.

"Any initiative that provides a way for members of the public to confirm their identity and age helping to prevent sales of age-restricted goods such as tobacco and alcohol to youngsters is to be welcomed."

Individuals can get more information or make an appointment for an identity card by calling 0300 330 0000.

4 Place a tick in the correct column for **each** of the six statements to show which are presented in Text B as facts and which are opinions.

	Fact	Opinion
Identity cards can be used in place of passports for travel in Europe.		
Many people under 30 lose their passports when using them as ID on a night out.		
Over 16,000 people have already registered an interest in getting an identity card on the Directgov website.		
The National Identity Card will be very useful for young people in London when buying age-restricted DVDs.		
Providing a way to prevent youngsters buying tobacco and alcohol is to be welcomed.		
Individuals can get more information about identity cards by calling 0300 330 0000.		

(3 marks)

5 Your friend is considering applying for a National Identity Card. Which **three** points in Text B do you think are the most important to convince them that it is a good idea?

You do **not** need to write in sentences.

i) ....

....

ii) ....

....

iii) ....

....

(3 marks)

6 According to Text B, how might the National Identity card be of benefit to convenience store owners?

(1 mark)

ResultsPlus
Top tip

4 At Level 2, you must recognise whether a statement is a fact or simply an opinion representing the viewpoint of the writer or another person. You will receive 1 mark for each **two** correctly placed ticks.

5 This question tests how well you can analyse the text and consider its suitability for a given purpose. You don't need to write in sentences but you should make sure each point is clearly stated. Look for three different points to make sure you get all of the three marks on offer.

6 This question is asking you to find specific information in the text. Think carefully about the question and make sure that your answer provides exactly the right information.

Read Text C and answer the questions which follow.

You have found a website advertising different cards that allow you to get discounts from a range of goods and services.

Text C

Address [ ] ⌄ → Go Links »

Young Person's Travel card

There are loads of discounts available in the UK and around the world, on all sorts of things – travel, shopping, cinema, restaurants.

And it's more than just a discount card – it gives you access to a 24 hour help line and a global SIM card for your mobile, so you can make all your calls using a UK number.

This card is available to EVERYONE UNDER 25. Minimum age 12. Your passport/driver's licence/birth certificate will be needed as proof of age.

It costs £12 for one year, or £30 for three years (only available for ages 12-23).

Student's Global Discount card

You can use this card in the UK and worldwide to make your money go further. Get discounts in hotels, museums, and loads of high-street stores, as well as special discounts for gigs and sporting events!

All this for only £10 per academic year.

If you're a full-time student doing 15 or more hours per week, for 12 weeks or more of the year then this is the card for you! You'll need to provide proof that you're a full time student from your place of study (gap year students need a document showing a confirmed UCAS placement for after your gap year) and proof of your age.

There is a minimum age of 12 but no maximum age.

Traveller's International Discount card

Want to travel the world but need to do it on a shoe-string? Only £15 a year will get you a Traveller's International Discount card and discounts on hostel accommodation in countries on every continent.

Great savings on travel, entertainment and adventure activities make sure your money goes as far as possible, and there are bonus features like travel assistance and free voice mail.

And anyone can buy one – it's available to all!

7 A member of your family has recently retired from work and now wants to travel round the world. Which of the three cards advertised in Text C would you recommend?

You do **not** need to write in sentences.

....

(1 mark)

ResultsPlus
Top tip

This question is asking you to solve a problem using the information in the text. Look for clues in the question to help you find the information you need for the correct answer.

8 Consider the information provided in the three adverts in Text C. Based on this information, which card do you think would be most suitable for you?

Give **three** reasons.

You do **not** need to write in sentences.

Card chosen ....

Reason 1 ....

Reason 2 ....

Reason 3 ....

(3 marks)

ResultsPlus
Top tip

This question is an open response – the answer will depend on your own preferences and situation. You do need to explain your decision though, by providing three reasons based on information in the text.

ResultsPlus
Self-assessment

1 When you have completed the questions in the Reading Test Zone, read the sample answers at 'pass' and 'fail' on the following pages. Use the comments from the examiner to help you to check what was required for each question.

2 Work on your own or with a partner to assess your own answers. For some questions, you will simply be able to check if your answers were right or wrong. For others, you need to read the different answers and decide which is most like your own.

3 When you have finished marking your answers, think about these questions:
   • What did you do well?
   • On what questions did your answer most closely match the 'fail' sample answer? What skills do you need to practice to improve those answers?

4 Set yourself an action plan to work towards a Level 2 pass for all questions.

On pages 40 to 45 you will find example 'pass' and 'fail' answers to the reading questions on pages 34 to 39. Read the aswers together with the examiner summaries to help you understand what is required to achieve a Level 2 pass.

Student 1 – extracts typical of 'pass Level 2' answers

1 What is the **main** purpose of Text A?

To give information about CitizenCard

(1 mark)

Examiner summary

The student has correctly viewed the text as a whole to work out the **main** purpose. 1 mark.

Answer Question 2 with a cross in the box (☒). If you change your mind about an answer, put a line through the box (☒) and then mark your new answer with a cross (☒).

2 Anyone signing documents to verify your identity must be:

☐	A	living at the same address
☐	B	working in any job
☒	C	25 years old or over
☐	D	closely related to you

(1 mark)

Examiner summary

The student has correctly identified the fact given in the text. By careful close reading they have avoided choosing answers with words that appear in the text but are not accurate. 1 mark.

3 Identify **two** reasons for buying a CitizenCard, according to Text A.

You do **not** need to write in sentences.

i) To prove who you are

ii) To prove your age

(2 marks)

Examiner summary

This is correct because the text states that you can do these things with a CitizenCard. The student has given the two points asked for. 2 marks.

4 Place a tick in the correct column for **each** of the six statements to show which are presented in Text B as facts and which are opinions.

	Fact	Opinion
Identity cards can be used in place of passports for travel in Europe.	✓	
Many people under 30 lose their passports when using them as ID on a night out.	✓	
Over 16,000 people have already registered an interest in getting an identity card on the Directgov website.	✓	
The National Identity Card will be very useful for young people in London when buying age-restricted DVDs.		✓
Providing a way to prevent youngsters buying tobacco and alcohol is to be welcomed.		✓
Individuals can get more information about identity cards by calling 0300 330 0000.	✓	

(3 marks)

Examiner summary

The student has correctly identified that facts are points of information stated by the text and supported by evidence. They have understood that point 4 is an opinion stated by the Home Office Minister because there is no evidence for this point. They have identified that point 5 is an opinion because it expresses a view about how people ought to feel. 3 marks.

5 Your friend is considering applying for a National Identity Card. Which **three** points in Text B do you think are the most important to convince them that it is a good idea?

You do **not** need to write in sentences.

i) You can use it instead of a passport in Europe

ii) It proves who you are so you don't need to carry your passport with you and risk losing it

iii) It means you're able to buy things if you need to be a certain age

(3 marks)

Examiner summary

This answer correctly gives three different valid reasons from Text B for buying a National Identity Card. The student could explain the difference between the first two reasons more clearly by noting that point one is about travel and point two is about identification once there, but gains marks for the right number of correct points. 3 marks

6 According to Text B, how might the National Identity card be of benefit to convenience store owners?

It will help them to make sure people are the right age to buy tobacco or alcohol

Examiner summary

The student has correctly identified and understood the relevant quotation in Text B from Suleman Khonat explaining that convenience store owners can ask to see the card if they want to check someone's age. 1 mark

7 A member of your family has recently retired from work and now wants to travel round the world. Which of the three cards advertised in Text C would you recommend?

You do **not** need to write in sentences.

The TID card is best because the other two are only for younger people or students

(1 mark)

Examiner summary

The student has read the question closely and explained that their choice is because the recommendation is for a retired person. 1 mark.

---

8 Consider the information provided in the three adverts in Text C. Based on this information, which card do you think would be most suitable for you?

Give **three** reasons.

You do **not** need to write in sentences.

Card chosen SGD card

Reason 1 I'm the right age for it

Reason 2 The discounts are on things I like doing

Reason 3 It's good value for £10

(3 marks)

Examiner summary

The student has identified acceptable reasons for buying the chosen card. They have given all the information asked for in the question. 3 marks

---

Student 2 – extracts typical of 'fail Level 2' answers

1 What is the **main** purpose of Text A?

To show you how to apply for a CitizenCard

(1 mark)

Examiner summary

This is only one of many pieces of information given and not the main purpose. If this was what the writer wanted to do, much of the text would be irrelevant – the **main** purpose should be supported by **most** of what the text is saying.

Answer Question 2 with a cross in the box (☒). If you change your mind about an answer, put a line through the box (☒) and then mark your new answer with a cross (☒).

2 Anyone signing documents to verify your identity must be:

☒	A	living at the same address
☐	B	working in any job
☐	C	25 years old or over
☐	D	closely related to you

(1 mark)

Examiner summary

The student has not read the text closely enough as it states that anyone signing the documents must **not** be living at the same address. Skimming the text to find where the information is given and then close reading it will help you to avoid this kind of mistake.

3 Identify **two** reasons for buying a CitizenCard, according to Text A.

You do **not** need to write in sentences.

i) To prove who you are

ii) Because anyone can get them at any age

(2 marks)

Examiner summary

The question asks for two reasons for buying a card, so you need to look for two **advantages** of having one. The first reason given is correct because in some situations you need to prove your identity so having a card would be of benefit. However, just being able to get a card is not a reason to have one unless the card helps you in some way. Always close read the question to be sure of exactly what you are being asked to do.

4 Place a tick in the correct column for **each** of the six statements to show which are presented in Text B as facts and which are opinions.

	Fact	Opinion
Identity cards can be used in place of passports for travel in Europe.		✓
Many people under 30 lose their passports when using them as ID on a night out.		✓
Over 16,000 people have already registered an interest in getting an identity card on the Directgov website.		✓
The National Identity Card will be very useful for young people in London when buying age-restricted DVDs.	✓	
Providing a way to prevent youngsters buying tobacco and alcohol is to be welcomed.	✓	
Individuals can get more information about identity cards by calling 0300 330 0000.		✓

(3 marks)

Examiner summary

The student has lost marks because they have not understood the differences between fact and opinion. Remember, facts are points that can be proven. Opinions are a person's viewpoint.

---

5 Your friend is considering applying for a National Identity Card. Which **three** points in Text B do you think are the most important to convince them that it is a good idea?

You do **not** need to write in sentences.

i) You can have one because you live in London

ii) It's only £30

iii) You can use it instead of your passport so you don't lose it

(3 marks)

Examiner summary

For this question, the student had to choose three convincing reasons for having a National Identity Card from the information and views given in Text B.
- Living in London means that the card would be available but is not sufficient reason to buy one because no benefit is given.
- A point about price is only valid if the card can be shown to represent good value and be cheaper than alternatives. There is no evidence given in the text about the cost of other types of identity card so this is not a valid answer.
- A mark would be allowed for the third reason given, but the student needs to describe how the card can be used instead of a passport (for example, to travel in Europe or as a form of identification) and explain clearly why it is safer and more convenient to carry the card.

---

6 According to Text B, how might the National Identity card be of benefit to convenience store owners?

It will help sales of alcohol ....

Examiner summary

The student has not understood or read carefully enough the point made about convenience store owners in the quotation by Suleman Khonat about preventing sales of alcohol and tobacco to under-age customers. The answer given here is incorrect because alcohol sales to under-age buyers would go down and sales to other people would not be affected.

7 A member of your family has recently retired from work and now wants to travel round the world. Which of the three cards advertised in Text C would you recommend?

You do **not** need to write in sentences.

The YPT card – retired person might need the help line ....

(1 mark)

Examiner summary

All the cards offer some benefits for travellers, so the correct answer will be the one most suitable for a retired person. This answer is incorrect because the YPT card is only available to people under 25 so the retired family member will not be able to buy one.

8 Consider the information provided in the three adverts in Text C. Based on this information, which card do you think would be most suitable for you?

Give **three** reasons.

You do **not** need to write in sentences.

Card chosen ..TID card...

Reason 1 It's the cheapest...

Reason 2 I'm the right age for it...

Reason 3 Good deal on voice mail..

(3 marks)

Examiner summary

Any choice of card is acceptable, but you must make sure that valid reasons are given. The student should look carefully at the advantages of each card and at the restrictions on who can buy them and compare the costs.
- The first reason is incorrect because the annual cost of a TID card is more than the other two. You might argue that it offers more benefits for the money and is therefore better value, but that is not the point made here.
- The second reason is correct but they should explain if they are not eligible for the other two cards. Anyone under 25 and over 12 is 'the right age' for any of the cards.
- The free voice mail is an acceptable reason.

Introduction to speaking, listening and communication

The activities in this section of the book will help you to develop your skills in contributing to discussions and making effective presentations.

- You will practise:
  - listening and responding
  - adapting your contributions
  - taking a range of roles in discussions.
- You will learn to present clearly and persuasively.
- At the end of the section you will find two speaking, listening and communication tasks to help you practise and assess the skills you will need to use in the assessment.
- There is also guidance from the examiner. For a full practice assessment, see pages 56–57.

Self-assessment

For each unit of work, you will be given learning objectives. Read these carefully before you start and work out how confident you feel about your skills in that area. At the end of each unit, think about how your skills have improved and what still needs further practice.

Your assessment

You will be assessed in your school or college, taking part in a discussion and a presentation. For more information on how you will be assessed, see pages 110–115.

This table shows you the 'standards', or assessment objectives, that your speaking, listening and communication will be assessed against.

Level 2 skill standard for speaking, listening and communication: Make a range of contributions to discussions in a range of contexts, including those that are unfamiliar, and make effective presentations.
Consider complex information and give a relevant, cogent response in appropriate language.
Present information and ideas clearly and persuasively to others.
Adapt contributions to suit audience, purpose and situation.
Make significant contributions to discussions, taking a range of roles and helping to move discussion forward.

Taking part in discussions

This lesson will help you to:
- plan and prepare a group discussion
- take a range of roles in a formal discussion.

Before you begin a discussion

Step 1 **Plan your contribution**

- Decide who you are discussing with.
  (For example, a meeting of staff and students.)

- Decide what your purpose is.
  (For example, to decide how to promote a school or college show.)

- Decide what kind of language would suit your audience and purpose.
  (For example, if the group's talk is part of a business meeting, you should use formal standard English.)

Step 2 **Prepare your points and arguments**

- Read through the information you are given and conduct further research if possible.

- Pick out the points that you will need to talk about in the discussion.

- Work out what you think about the topic.

- Make a plan showing the points you want to be covered in the discussion.

Activity 1

1 You are going to take part in a formal group discussion; read the details given below.

2 Make notes for this discussion; remember to follow the points listed in Step 1 above.

Situation
The government is considering whether all 14-year-olds should be given parenting lessons in school and if so, what these lessons should include. You have been asked to join a student focus group to discuss this and give your views. You have been given the information opposite as a starting point.

Top tip
Research your material well before the discussion. This will give you confidence, which will give your comments more authority. Make sure you have thought through your own ideas on the subject too.

Activity 2

2 **a** Read the information and opinions in Texts A to G opposite. Decide what you agree with or disagree with.

   b Make a plan showing the points you want to make during the discussion. Use points from the information opposite, as well as your own ideas.

3 Swap your spider diagram with a partner. Make a note of two points your partner wants to make which will contradict or oppose your points. Work out how you can argue against them.

Text A

- Britain has the highest teenage pregnancy rate in Europe.
- Every day, 22 girls under-15 become pregnant.
- In Lewisham, London, 1 in 62 girls under-16 becomes pregnant.
- In the Cotswolds, 1 in 556 girls under-16 becomes pregnant.
- 12,000 men under-20 become fathers every year.

Text B

'I am struggling to think why we need parenting education as young as 14. This is in danger of institutionalising teenage pregnancy and could create an interest where none existed.'

Margaret Morrissey, spokesperson for Parents Outloud

Text C

'We shouldn't waste valuable lesson time on this when fewer than half our teenagers leave school with 5 A–C Grade GCSEs. The money for teenage parenting lessons should be used for getting them the qualifications that will guarantee a good job and a bright future.'

Lisa Taylor, Parent

Text D

'It's true that teenage parenting lessons may be forgotten by the time many become parents, but anything is better than doing nothing and letting babies grow up damaged and unable to succeed in life because their mother or father hadn't got a clue what to do.'

Dave Watkins, Teacher

Text E

Possible teenage parenting course content

- the role and responsibilities of being a parent
- the importance of emotional security
- ways in which parents can influence their children's future success
- basic techniques for keeping children out of trouble
- relationships: handling conflict.

Text F

Teenagers only live for the moment, but having a child is for life

Text G

'It's a big responsibility because the baby is completely dependent on you for everything. With no job, no money and no idea how to look after a baby it's a big shock. You really feel on your own and you have to learn everything for yourself. It's scary.'

JP, Teenage dad

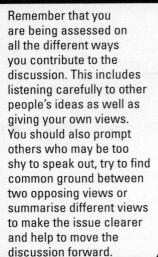

In a group of four, study the information below about how to work successfully together in your group, then decide what **you** need to remember to do most.

Step 3 Succeeding as a group member

▶ Decide what roles are needed in your group and who will fill them. For example, chairperson (runs the meeting, ensures everyone sticks to the point and sums up at the end), scribe (keeps clear notes of all key points and decisions), timekeeper (monitors the time and moves the discussion on if necessary so that it does not run over the time allowed).

▶ Treat each person's ideas as worth considering.

▶ Make sure that everyone has a chance to speak. Ask each other questions and answer each other. If someone in your group is holding back, draw them in to the discussion. For example, look at them and ask, 'What do you think?' or 'Do you agree?'

▶ Show that you are listening when someone is speaking. Make eye contact and nod if you agree with the point they are making.

▶ Prepare to respond to what people say with relevant ideas and reasons. Use the ideas below.

▶ Make sure that decisions are reached and are group decisions, based on reasons and argument.

If you don't understand something, ask questions like:

Why?   What do you mean?   Can you explain?

If you agree, give your reasons and add a similar point or evidence, using words like:

I agree, because...   Another point supporting that is...   Similarly...   In addition...

Use the speaker's own words in your response to show that you agree.

If you disagree, politely challenge the speaker's views. Explain your point of view using words like:

However...   On the other hand...   Alternatively...   I disagree, because...

Show that everyone's view is valued, using words like:

That's an interesting viewpoint...

Help your group make good progress. Use these words and phrases:

We need to stay on task.   To summarise...   We need to move on...

In conclusion...   Are we all agreed?

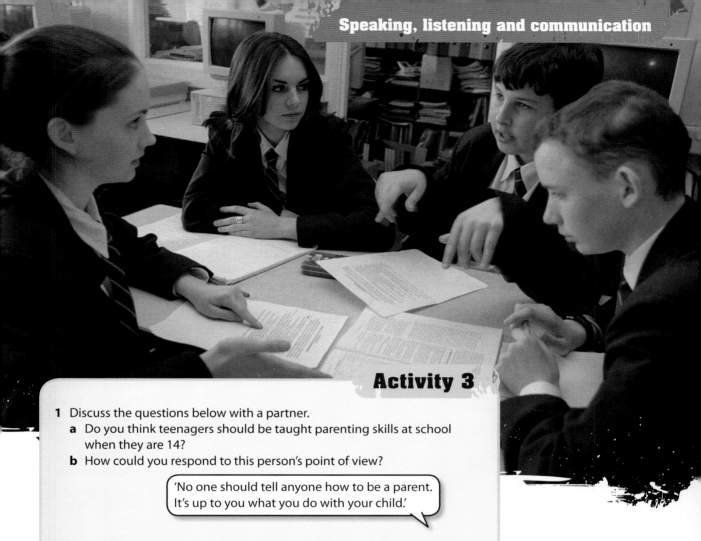

Activity 3

1 Discuss the questions below with a partner.
   a Do you think teenagers should be taught parenting skills at school when they are 14?
   b How could you respond to this person's point of view?

> 'No one should tell anyone how to be a parent. It's up to you what you do with your child.'

2 Now, take turns to share your responses to the questions above. Remember to use the discussion skills described on the page opposite.

3 In your discussion group, spend 5 minutes discussing the issues. Use all that you have learned so far to keep the discussion moving.

4 With a partner, decide:
   a how your group is getting on.
   b what the group needs to do to move forward to a decision.

5 In your group again, share your thoughts about how the discussion is going and what you need to do now. Make notes to help you stay focused.

6 Continue your formal discussion. Reach a final decision about whether 14-year-olds should be given parenting lessons in schools and if so, what the lessons should include.

   Use all the skills you have been developing during this unit.

7 **a** By yourself, reflect on how well you contributed to the discussion. Look back at the steps 1–3 on pags 49 and 50. Which things did you do well? What could you improve next time?
   b Share your ideas with the rest of the group. Listen to each other and then help each person to set a goal for improvement next time you have a group discussion. Together, draw up a checklist of tips for each of the roles you might take in a discussion.

Making effective presentations

This lesson will help you to:
- plan, prepare and give a well-organised presentation tailored to your audience
- listen carefully and respond to questions from your audience.

You are going to make a formal presentation. Read the details given below.

Situation
You are taking part in a research project on how students can use the internet to help students to save money. You have been asked to give a presentation to recommend a website that could do this. Your audience could be **either** other students **or** their parents.

Step 1 Start to plan your presentation
- Work out answers to these questions:
  - What is your presentation going to be about? (For example, using *lastfm.com* instead of spending money on *iTunes* downloads.)
  - Who is your audience and how much do they know already? (For example, students probably already know about *iTunes*, but might not use *lastfm.com*. However, parents may need explanations of both.)
  - What will your audience want to find out? (For example, students may want lots of details of what the site does, but parents will want an introduction to the main features.)
  - What is your purpose? (For example, to entertain, persuade, inform, instruct?)
- Decide how you will open and close your presentation, and the timings for each of the sections in between.

Activity 2

Put your ideas into a table like the one below.

My presentation is about:	
My audience wants to know:	
On the site you can:	

Step 2 Prepare and plan your points and arguments

▶ Use the checklist on the right to help you work out what to include.

▶ Make your presentation more interesting by including some amusing stories or surprising information. For example, if you are a musician you can upload your songs to build a fanbase on *lastfm.com* – and you'll be paid royalties if people listen to your music.

▶ Learn the information under each heading on your plan. Practise saying it.

Reasons for your choice of website.
- How often you visit the website and why.
- Different things the website allows visitors to do.
- How the website attracts visitors.
- What makes it better than other similar websites.

Activity 3

1 Put your ideas from Step 2 into a flowchart. Make brief notes under each heading to use as a plan to jog your memory as you speak.

2 Add some reasons for your ideas to your notes.

3 Note where you could use some of the words and phrases in the box below to link your ideas or add examples and evidence.

To add points, use:	also too in addition similarly in the same way as like
To contrast points, use:	but however although though on the other hand in contrast
To explain points, use:	therefore so then as a result this shows that
To give examples or evidence, use:	for example for instance to prove this point

Step 3 Preparing and using visual aids

▶ Think about how you can display your website as a visual aid. For example, you could project it onto a whiteboard or print out an enlarged version of part of it.

Top tip

As you plan what to include, check that everything is relevant to what you have been asked to do.

Remember

Visual aids can be distracting if:

▶ The audience focuses on them more than on what you are saying.

▶ You forget to keep looking at your audience.

▶ You read what is on them rather than using them to make a point.

▶ You lose track of what you are saying because you are dealing with the visual aid.

Only use visual aids if you are sure they will add to the effectiveness of your presentation.

Activity 4

1 Decide when you will refer to your visual aid in your presentation and put a reminder on your plan.

2 Practise using visual aids effectively.

Step 4 Using the right language

▶ Be polite and mature.

▶ Use formal standard English.

▶ Sound enthusiastic and positive – your audience will enjoy your presentation much more.

Activity 5

1 With a partner, take turns to run through your presentation using standard English. Your partner must say 'Stop!' every time you use non-standard English, for example slang or dialect words. Together work out what you should have said instead and try again, using the new phrase.

2 Learn your new phrases, then attempt the same task with a different partner, trying to include your improvements.

Step 5 Practise your presentation

When you speak in front of a group:

▶ act confidently, even if you're not – just as many actors, politicians and celebrities do

▶ stand still and stand up straight

▶ speak more loudly, more slowly and more clearly than you would normally

▶ keep your audience involved and make eye contact with different listeners, and vary your tone of voice

▶ consider when and how you will deal with questions.

Activity 6

1 Practise giving your presentation several times to your group, friends or family, or in front of a mirror at home. If you can, record yourself speaking so that you can listen to your presentation and work out ways to improve it.

2 Ask listeners for feedback. For example, ask 'Can you hear me?'; 'Am I speaking too fast?'; 'Does it make sense when I say...?' You could also gather written feedback.

3 Time yourself. Decide what to leave out if your presentation is too long, or add some more points if it is too short. You should aim for between 10 and 15 minutes.

Step 6 Give your presentation

Read the pointers below and use them to help you give
your presentation.

▶ Try to be clear, calm and confident. Overcome nerves by breathing
in and out slowly before you start.

▶ Act as though you are the world's best presenter, with lots of energy.

▶ If a problem occurs, no one else knows what was meant to happen
– so just keep going.

▶ Tell your audience whether you will be answering questions during
your presentation or at the end.

▶ Listen carefully to any questions and answer as best you can.

▶ If you don't know the answer, say so, but offer to look it up later.

▶ Make a note of any questions so that you do not forget.

Watch out!

Try not to rush – give your
audience time to take
in what you are saying.
Think of your audience
as individual people and
make sure each one
feels included. Make eye
contact and ensure they
can all see and hear you.

Activity 7

1 Remind yourself of all the advice in this section and check your plan.

2 Give your presentation.

3 Afterwards, make notes on what went well and what you can improve
next time.

Step 7 Listen to and respond to other people's presentations

▶ Be the kind of audience you would
like to speak in front of. Look
interested, make eye contact with
the speaker and pay attention.

▶ Notice the things each speaker does
well. This can be a good way to learn
to be a better presenter.

▶ Remember to praise other speakers
and show that you were listening to
them, for example 'I was impressed
by what you said about…'

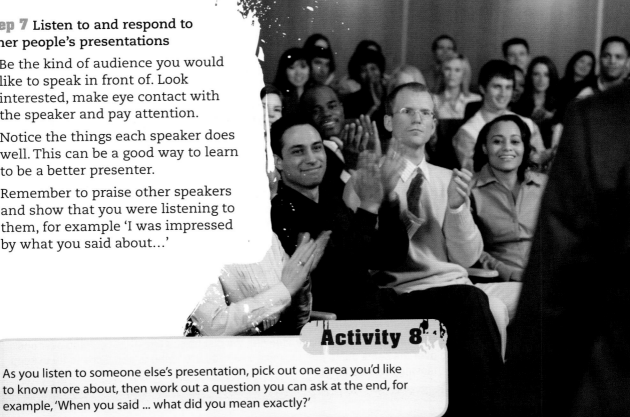

Activity 8

As you listen to someone else's presentation, pick out one area you'd like
to know more about, then work out a question you can ask at the end, for
example, 'When you said … what did you mean exactly?'

Speaking, listening and communication practice tasks

▶ Look at the examples of the kinds of tasks you may be given in your speaking, listening and communication assessments.

▶ Use the examiner's tips and the self-assessment checklist on pages 58–59 to develop your skills in taking part in discussions and making presentations.

Discussion

Local residents have been calling for a youth dispersal order in your area. This would give the police powers to ask children and young people to move on after 9pm if they believe them to be at risk of committing crime or anti-social behaviour.

You have been asked to join a student focus group to discuss this issue. The aim is to give your views so that the local council can consider them before making a decision. You should discuss, in a group of five or six, whether you feel there is a need for a youth dispersal order in your area. Try to consider a range of views in your discussion. Use the speech bubbles below to help you.

> I own the late night convenience store and I definitely think we need a dispersal order. Teenagers hanging around late at night scare my customers off.

> I've lived in this area safely for 46 years but now I'm scared to go out at night. The big noisy gangs of teenagers make me feel very nervous.

> We should think about what teenagers need instead of just blaming them for everything – my own kids wouldn't hang around at night if they had something better to do.

> I don't think we need this order. Yes, we hang around in the evenings. But we aren't harming anyone or committing crimes. We're just having a laugh.

Top tip

- Make sure you are clear on your audience and purpose — and what kind of language you should use.
- Prepare the points you want to cover. Do some research on the Internet, if you need to. What is your own view?

In a successful discussion, everyone must play a part. At different times, you can:

- start the discussion – organise the group or help to plan the task
- develop the discussion – ask questions or for a point to be explained
- suggest alternative ideas
- lead the discussion – act as chairperson, summarise views and help to resolve conflicts.

Give your own views clearly, concisely and persuasively, but also listen carefully to what others have to say. Don't let the discussion get stuck by going over and over the same point. Keep in mind what you are trying to achieve and try to keep moving towards that goal.

Presentation

Your school or college is taking part in a project to help local people to understand more about environmental issues. Plan and give a presentation arguing for or against the idea that recycling is essential for the future of our planet. Aim to speak for about 10 minutes. Use the prompts below to help you.

Recycling helps to save precious resources and reduce the output of harmful chemicals. We all have a responsibility to do what we can to help.

Metals, such as drinks cans, can be recycled without losing any of their properties – so they're as good as new when reused. This has enormous environmental benefits. Recycling metals:
- reduces water pollution and air emissions
- saves on raw materials, such as iron ore, aluminium and coal
- uses much less energy than making new material
- reduces waste.

Some people say domestic recycling is not worth the time and effort it takes. According to recent statistics, only 2% of metal recycled in the UK comes from household recycling. Even if we managed to increase our household recycling by 50%, the total amount of waste going to landfill would only be reduced by 5%.

Recycling costs money and car journeys to recycling collection points add to the carbon emissions polluting the atmosphere. Perhaps we should be concentrating on using less instead – then we wouldn't have so much to throw away.

Top tip

- Make sure you are clear on your audience and purpose, and what kind of language you should use.
- Decide if you are going to argue for or against the idea that recycling is essential.
- Make sure you understand the opposite viewpoint and be able to say why you don't agree with it.
- To persuade others to your point of view, you need to collect as much reliable evidence as you can. Prepare the points you want to cover – do some research on the internet if necessary.
- Include some surprising facts if you can, to make your presentation interesting.
- Don't rely on multimedia projections or whiteboards, etc. Use them to support and illustrate the points you make as a presenter but don't let them become a distraction.
- Rehearse your presentation aloud. Get someone to time you and give you feedback.
- Notes are useful, but don't just read from a prepared script.
- Speak slowly and clearly, look at your audience and try to relax!

Self-assessment

1. When you have completed the discussion and presentation tasks on pages 56–57, reflect on your own performance. Use the tips from the examiner to help you.

2. On your own or with a partner, use the checklist opposite to mark your performance. To achieve a Level 2 for your speaking, listening and communication, you need to be able to say 'Yes' to most or all of the points on the checklist.

3. Help each other to set goals for improvement:

   * Where you ticked 'sometimes', think about the times that you did not demonstrate the skill. What can you do to improve?

   For example, if your use of visual aids distracted your audience, think about how you could use them more effectively. Plan to practise your presentations using the visual aids, so that you get feedback on how you can improve.

   * Where you ticked 'no', set yourself the goal of practising the skill. Review the relevant parts of pages 46–57. Try practising the skill informally.

   For example, if you used too much slang, ask a partner to listen to you and put their hand up every time you do so. Then think of a better word you could use. Keep practising until you are confident of the skill.

Self-assessment checklist

	Yes	Sometimes	No
Do I show I have been listening carefully by linking my own comments and questions clearly to what others have said?			
Do I use the correct scientific or technical terms where necessary and avoid using slang terms which might not be understood by everyone?			
Can I explain my ideas clearly so my audience understands and is persuaded to share my views?			
Can I use visual aids, such as PowerPoint, to support my presentation without replacing or weakening my own role in it?			
Can I match my words, volume and tone of voice to suit the age, level of confidence, ability and knowledge of my audience?			
In discussions, do I pay attention to others' views and what the group is trying to achieve?			
Can I make and explain relevant points clearly?			
Do I encourage others to put their views forward and support their ideas by comments, questions or non-verbal means?			
Can I help to keep discussions moving forward towards a decision and to resolve disagreements within the group?			
Can I confidently participate in discussions, including those with people I am unfamiliar with? For example: • presenting my own ideas clearly • listening attentively • encouraging and supporting others • negotiating • leading • record-keeping			

Introduction to writing

The texts and activities in this section of the book will help you to develop your skills for writing a range of texts to communicate information, ideas and opinions.

- You will:
  - think about audience, purpose, form and style
  - learn how to organise and present your writing clearly, logically, effectively and persuasively.
- You will be given guidance to help you make sure that your spelling, punctuation and grammar are accurate and clear.
- At the end of the section you will find two writing tasks to help you practise and assess your writing skills in the kinds of questions you will meet in the test.
- There are also sample answers at Pass and Fail, with comments from the examiner. For a full practice test, see pages 127–28.

ResultsPlus
Self-assessment

For each unit of work, you will be given learning objectives. Read these carefully before you start and work out how confident you feel about your skills in that area. At the end of each unit, think about how your skills have improved and what still needs further practice.

Your assessment

You will be assessed in one 45-minute test, with two writing tasks. For more information on how you will be assessed, see pages 110–115.

This table shows you the 'standards', or assessment objectives, that your work will be assessed against in your writing test.

Level 2 skill standard for writing: Write a range of texts, including extended written documents, communicating information, ideas and opinions effectively and persuasively.
Present information/ideas concisely, logically and persuasively.
Present information on complex subjects clearly and concisely.
Use a range of writing styles for different purposes.
Use a range of sentence structures, including complex sentences, and paragraphs to organise written communication effectively.
Punctuate written text using commas, apostrophes and inverted commas accurately.
Ensure written work is fit for purpose and audience, with accurate spelling and grammar that support clear meaning in a range of text types.

Planning your writing: a summary

Use the grid below to help you as you work through the tasks in this Writing section and in your assessments. It will help you to plan an effective piece of writing.

Purpose Your purpose could be to:	Key words The task might use words such as:	Format You might be asked to write a:
instruct/advise/ request	telling, asking, reserving, booking, ordering, inviting, suggesting	notice leaflet letter e-mail
inform/explain	informing, presenting, explaining, announcing, describing, communicating, notifying, stating, suggesting	leaflet letter e-mail article
argue	arguing, protesting, disagreeing, challenging, complaining , requesting	letter article leaflet
discuss	discussing, examining, commenting, reviewing, helping to decide, recommending	briefing paper
		article
		report
persuade	convincing, persuading, giving your opinion, winning support for your viewpoint	leaflet
		advertisement
		speech, podcast, article

For any writing task you are given:

▶ first identify the words in the task that show the purpose by using column 1. For example, if the question uses the word 'telling' your purpose may be to instruct
▶ then check what format to write in (some examples are given in column 3)
▶ practise using the features given in column 4 to plan and shape your text.

| **Features** |
| Remember to include these features: |

Title: state what you are writing about
Main section: write clearly your purpose and relevant information
Without forgetting: appropriate layout features for letters

Title: state what you are writing about and why
Introduction: to the topic
Main section: explain the steps in a logical order – how and why things happen as they do – with subheadings. You may use bulleted or numbered lists
Conclusion: to sum up the explanation

Title: state what is being discussed
Introduction: to the issues involved and your viewpoint
Arguments: for your viewpoint, with reasons, evidence and examples
Answers: to any arguments against your viewpoint, with reasons, evidence and examples
Conclusion: to sum up your viewpoint and arguments

Title: a question to sum up the topic
The issue: what the paper is for and why
Background: information, history, explanation
Considerations: a list of facts showing both sides
Analysis: things to be considered
Conclusion: to sum up the findings and make recommendations

Title: a headline to sum up the topic
Introduction: use a statement or question to set the scene and focus on the topic
Main section: detailed examples and comments
Conclusion/recommendations: what you think should happen (for the reader to consider)

Title: statement or question to engage reader in your topic and purpose
Introduction: state the subject and purpose of the report
Main section: logical grouping of information, with subheadings. May use bulleted or numbered lists
Conclusion/recommendations: summarise the report's findings
and suggest actions

Title: 'what' identified
Main section: writer's viewpoint and relevant information with evidence. May use bulleted or numbered lists
Conclusion: urge the audience to take action

Title: state what you are writing about in an interesting way
Main section: appeal to the audience's wants, needs, wishes. Include a memorable slogan. Make claims for the product or service.
Conclusion: urge the audience to take action

Introduction: state your viewpoint
Main section: order points supporting your viewpoint. Give evidence and examples
Conclusion: memorable closing statement of your point of view

Before writing, always read the task carefully and find the key words which tell you:

▶ exactly what you have to write

▶ who it is for – your audience.

For example:

> What you have to write   The audience
>
> Write **a letter** to **the chairperson of your local council**, persuading them to create better leisure facilities for residents of your age.

ResultsPlus
Top tip

When you plan your writing, remember to include a note about the audience for the writing task. Use this as a guide for what you say and the way you express yourself. Ask yourself, 'What do they need to know and what is the most effective way to tell them?'

Now think about what your audience is like and what they need to know, for example:

> Chairperson – likely to be older and quite formal. Needs to know what people my age want to do for leisure and why they should provide it.

Finally, decide how you will suit the content and style of your writing to the audience, for example:

> I need to use formal standard English so the council leader will take me seriously and understand what I have to say. I need to give clear detailed explanations with sound and persuasive reasons.

Activity 1

1 Who is the audience for each of the four writing tasks below?
   a You have a friend who has owed you money for several weeks and wants to borrow more from you. Write an email to your friend, explaining why you are unwilling to lend him or her £150 to buy a mobile phone.
   b Should advertising of fast food be banned during children's television programmes? Write your view as a contribution to a discussion on a parenting website.
   c Write a letter to the catering manager of the canteen you use at school, college or work, explaining how they could improve the service and meals on offer.
   d You have completed a sponsored swim as part of a fundraising event. Write an article about the experience for a local newspaper.

2 Complete a table like the one below for each of the four tasks. Work out what the audience is like and what they need from your writing.

	Task's audience	What the task tells you about the audience	Educated guess: what the audience is like	What does the audience need?
a				
b				
c				
d				

3 For each task, explain how you would make sure your content and style are suited to the audience.

4 **a** Read the task below and decide how you would suit the content and style of your writing to the audience.

> Write a report to inform your school's management team of your views on how better use could be made of technology such as mobile phones, laptops, a virtual learning environment or other technology, to improve students' learning.

   b Surinder and Ben have both started work on the task. Ben has written a final draft, matching his writing carefully to the audience. Surinder has jotted down some of his ideas before starting his draft. Suggest how Surinder could draft ideas to suit the audience for his writing.

Surinder
It's cool using Facebook, Twitter, texts and emails but can they help you learn? I reckon. It would be good fun and everyone would turn up to lessons so that would improve learning to start with.

Ben
Technology is part of everyone's life but especially students and business people. Using technology in lessons prepares students for future life and because it's enjoyable it's also motivating. I can't think of a lesson that wouldn't be better with PowerPoints, or research that wouldn't be helped by internet access.

5 Draft a paragraph of your own for this task. Then swap with a partner and discuss how well you have tailored your writing for its audience.

ResultsPlus
Top tip

Read the task carefully and think about what your writing needs to achieve. You could lose marks if you don't, because your response could be irrelevant or written in the wrong style.

What you write and how you write it should help you achieve your purpose. To work out the purpose:

▶ Read the task and find the key words which tell you about your purpose for writing (for example, inform, persuade, explain).

▶ Work out what content your writing should have to achieve its purpose (for example, facts, evidence).

▶ Decide what style you need to use (for example, formal standard English, rhetorical questions, facts, opinions).

▶ Decide what presentation features to include (for example, paragraphs, bullet points and lists, persuasive techniques).

Use the grid of text types on pages 62–63 to help you.

Activity 1

1 Read the tasks below and identify the purpose of each one.

   a Write a letter persuading the head teacher of your school or college to introduce a new sport of your choice into the curriculum.

   b Your local newspaper has been running a series of articles about road safety. Write an article for the newspaper, discussing whether the legal age for driving should be raised to 21.

   c Write a report for your local council on what facilities young adults in your area need in order to live a healthier lifestyle.

   d Write an article for your school's website, arguing for or against the use of social networking sites by teenagers.

   e Write an email to a holiday company, suggesting ways in which they could make sure their new holiday resort appeals to families with teenagers and younger chidren.

2 Decide what features you should include in your writing for each task. Use the grid on pages 62–63 to help you.

3 Tunmise has discussed Task E with other students, and has jotted down some ideas.

Plan

Ideas
Trendy room designs, laptop and wifi in each room
Wii and TV in each room
Bar for teenagers and nightclub open till 3.00am
Karaoke machines
Youth lounge to chill out in with music, sofas, drinks, pool table, games tables
TV screens with sport and music channels in the restaurant

Style
Write in informal English, use slang so reader knows I'm cool and the right
person to be telling them how to design their hotel.

Presentation
Set it out like a business letter so they have got my home address to write
back to me.
Bullet points, text boxes for different ideas.

Tunmise now wants to review her ideas and consider how to make sure her
email will be more effective in achieving its purpose. Think about what she
should write and how she should write it. Use the grid on pages 62–63 to
help you.

4 Make a plan for Task A. Decide what content to include and how you will
write so that your text will achieve its purpose.

Different texts are laid out in a range of ways and include different features. For example, a report usually has headings, subheadings and paragraphs, but a formal letter has two addresses, the date, a greeting and salutation. Always:

▶ read the task carefully and pinpoint which form your text should be written in

▶ include the correct features of that form when writing your text.

Activity 1

1 Study texts A to E on pages 69–73. They are all about the Duke of Edinburgh's Award, but they are written in different forms. For each one:
   a Write down the name of the form.
   b Copy out and complete the labels to make a list of features to include when writing in that form.

2 Use your notes to make a revision card of what to include when writing in each form. Include checklists, and diagrams of features.

> Form: formal letter
>
> Has two addresses:
> • mine top right with the date under it
> • the reader's below on the left.

3 Learn your checklists, then work with a partner and test each other.

Text A: Report

[Title tells readers...]

[Tense mainly ...]

[Images and graphics to...]

Money matters

This year we have supported 275,000 young people with total expenditure of around £6m. We achieve this impact by working with a very strong network of partners and volunteers, who together contribute many times more than this to our cause.

[Introduction tells readers...]

Where the money comes from

Our three main sources of income for the charity are donations and grants, fundraising events, and trading income from operations, literature and merchandise sales. We work hard to maximise the return from each of these sources.

- Over **80% of income** from donations and grants goes to charitable purposes.
- For every **£1** we spend on fundraising events, we receive **£1.83** of income. Our fundraising events are self-financing.

This year we raised a total of **£6.22m** net to spend on our Charity's work.

[Facts and evidence to...]

Where the money goes

Enabling more young people to access our programmes: £1,771k

We aim to make sure every young person has the ability to access our programmes, regardless of background or barriers.

This part of our work supports our activity with excluded and vulnerable young people, as well as setting up new groups and supporting the recruitment of new young people to our programmes.

[Subheadings tell readers...]

[Paragraphs are used for...]

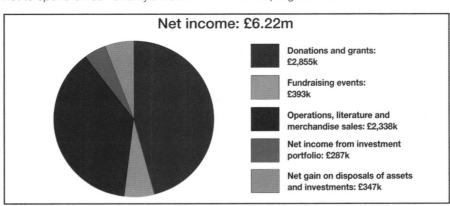

Net income: £6.22m

Donations and grants: £2,855k

Fundraising events: £393k

Operations, literature and merchandise sales: £2,338k

Net income from investment portfolio: £287k

Net gain on disposals of assets and investments: £347k

DofE Annual Review 2008

Text B: Briefing paper

A briefing paper is for a particular audience. it should take into account their needs and …

Briefing paper for Board of Governors

Should our school run the Duke of Edinburgh Award?

Title sums up the … of the briefing paper.

Subheadings are used to…

Issue

Many schools already offer the Duke of Edinburgh (DofE) Award to students as an extra-curricular activity. Currently we do not. This means students at our school may be missing out on a valuable experience.

Issue — sum up in a couple of sentences what … and why the audience…

Background

DofE programmes are for 14–19-year-olds. Awards are achieved by completing a personal programme of activities and all activities must be completed before student's 25th birthday. There are three levels: Bronze, Silver and Gold. The four categories that have to be completed for Bronze and Silver are: Volunteering, Physical, Skills, Expedition. For Gold a Residential category has to be completed. A huge variety of activities is possible within each category. Each stage done in turn takes at least 6 months, but if a stage is done singly then it's 6 months for Bronze, 12 months for Silver and 18 months for Gold. Students keep a record book so they can complete their programme elsewhere if necessary.

Background — give information, history, and explanations that will help the reader…

Considerations

Considerations — list…

Priorities
- To develop the range of out of hours school activities to make the school attractive to all students.

Different ways of presenting key information…

Pros
- DofE offers something for everyone.
- It is highly valued by Further Education colleges, universities and employers.
- It develops students' characters and life skills — and broadens their outlook.
- It is very motivating for students and generates good publicity for the school.
- It's a well-developed organisation, with lots of resources and back-up via website.
- It fits in with the school's values and ethos.

Cons
- Staff commitment – needs a course leader and other staff to support activities. The time staff have to give is high, especially for expeditions.
- Cost – each student pays £11.50 for Bronze and Silver, £17.25 to participate in Gold. Additional costs depend on students' choice of activities.
- Additional use of our minibus which is already in great demand for sports events.

Options

We could link in with another current provider to share costs and skills.

Conclusion — this should…

Conclusion

DofE is a well-established and highly valued course which would benefit many different students. A questionnaire could find out how many students would like to take part. The costs are a concern, but the option of linking with another provider to share costs is a possibility to investigate.

Text C: Magazine article

Image to...

Heading tells ... and grabs readers' interest by...

Opening paragraph grabs readers' attention by ... and tells readers...

eDofE: FUTURE PRESENT

The new online system for recording participants' progress through their DofE programmes – *eDof*E – was made fully available last September. Here's a rundown of how it works and some popular questions are answered...

In the first three months since *e*DofE went live we had over 23,500 young people using *e*DofE and working through their DofE programmes. These young people are being supported by 70 regional staff, 414 Operating Authorities and 1,000 Operating Authority staff. They are managing the DofE process online and rising to the challenge of working in a fresh, new and exciting environment.

There have been over 80 training courses held around the UK which is giving the system a good workout in real-life situations.

Subheadings used to...

Challenges

As with all things new there have been a few hiccups on the way from a system perspective. We have to thank everyone concerned who has risen to the challenge when this has occurred and still achieved the objectives of delivering training courses with satisfied delegates.

We have been reviewing the calls logged to the help desk (0845 467 0487) and put together the top issues that have been raised during September and October regarding the use of *e*DofE:

"I can't log on – help!" It can take up to 25 seconds for the system to load up when you first log on. By this time some may try to log on again, thinking there is some kind of error. This invokes a one minute penalty before you can log on again. Do this five times and you are locked out for up to 30

DofE magazine - issue 5 Spring 2010

minutes. The advice is to be patient and watch the progress bar at the bottom of your screen.

"Someone has forgotten their user name or password" At the moment only System Administrators can re-set user names and passwords so you will need to call/email Windsor (**eDofE@DofE.org**). This will shortly be delegated to Managers/Leaders.

"The system has saved an address that is not mine!" This was a bug in the address validation system which has now been sorted out and address validation is now working perfectly.

"I miss the old *Record Books*" An integral part of *e*DofE is the production of a good quality bound book, containing the information – Assessors' comments, participant's reports, photographs etc. – that has been uploaded to a participant's *e*DofE area. This will form a more comprehensive, smart memento of

a young person's DofE journey than the *Record Book*. Work is nearing completion on this *Achievement Pack* and its availability will be announced in *e*DofE.

What is next?

We are busy finalising the feedback received from the field and working our way through the list of enhancements to phase one of the system. These include small changes to elements such as buttons, options and menus up to more significant changes such as allowing a young person to change their activity whilst still recording their progress. Other significant work packages include the finalisation of the reporting suite, completing the *Achievement Pack* and working with partners on how we can get our systems to interface fully with each other.

All in all we have had a fantastic launch, thanks largely to the support of the users, and look forward to improving our system to support young people to achieve their goals.

More information, user guides and support can be obtained from **www.DofE.org/eDofE**

> *In the afternoon we set up all staff members on the system. No problems. They have phoned me since and remain enthusiastic.*
> Geoff Price, Leader

> *I really enjoy using eDofE!*
> Zsofia Participant

> *I have this evening been doing a group eDofE training session in Bournemouth, it went exceptionally well and they loved it.*
> Helen Carby
> Development Officer, South West

Quotations used to...

Concluding sentence leaves readers with a final point to...

Page 29

Includes writer's viewpoints and comments supported by...

Includes different people's experiences...

Points made in each paragraph are in .... order

Link to further information

Text D: Persuasive text

Heading tells reader … and grabs attention by…

Opening statement tells reader…

Writer's viewpoint supported by facts, opinions, evidence

Images and graphics to…

Powerful descriptive words and verbs and emotive language used to …

Directly addresses reader to…

Rhetorical questions used to…

Memorable closing statement to…

Save the Children
Student Enterprise Scheme

Now an Approved Activity Provider!

As part of our Student Enterprise Scheme you'll be supporting our work and making a real difference to children's lives while you develop your skills and hopefully have fun!

- Develop a business.
- Organise and publicise a fundraising event.
- Co-ordinate a campaign.

You choose!

Gain skills in:

- Marketing
- Event management
- Media and publicity
- Campaigning
- Leadership and team work
- Finance and business sense

Learn more about:

- How charities work
- Your power to change the world
- The impact of your support
- How to make your voice heard

The Best Bit...

Save the Children has just become an Approved Activity Provider under the volunteering section so taking part in our Student Enterprise Scheme will help you to fulfil the volunteer criteria of your Duke of Edinburgh's Award. Sound good?

We Save the Children Will you?

DE APPROVED ACTIVITY PROVIDER

For more information call the Schools and Youth Team at Save the Children on 020 7012 6400 or visit our website savethechildren.org.uk/enterprise to register for your student enterprise pack.

We're the world's independent children's charity. We're outraged that millions of children are still denied proper healthcare, food, education and protection. We're working flat out to get every child their rights and we're determined to make further, faster changes. How many? How fast? It's up to you.

Save the Children® Registered charity England and Wales (213890) Scotland (SC039570).

...azine - issue 5 Spring 2010

Text E: Formal letter

Your address on the…

24 Eden Grove
Walmsley
Essex
21st March 2010

Place the date…

Reader's name and address are placed…

Ms J Sandhu
Human Resources Officer
The Duke of Edinburgh's Award
Gulliver House
Madeira Walk
Windsor SL4 1EU

The greeting is placed…

Dear Ms J Sandhu,

Use 'Dear' + name when…
Use 'Dear Sir' or 'Dear Madam' when…

The opening sentence tells the reader why…

I should like to apply for the post of Young Person's Support Officer as advertised on the Duke of Edinburgh Award website on 2nd Feb 2010. Please find enclosed my CV giving my details as requested. As you will see I have extensive experience of working with young people in this area and would welcome the opportunity to contribute to the welfare of young people. I look forward to hearing from you.

The last sentence should express what response the writer…

Yours sincerely,

Rhia Williams

Sign your name…

Place the salutation…
Use 'Yours sincerely' when…
Use 'Yours faithfully' when…

Activity 2

1 Read the tasks below. Decide and write down what form you would need to use for each task.
   a Write a one-page leaflet persuading members of your school or college to recycle.
   b Write a persuasive letter to your local MP, arguing that schools, colleges and universities should offer courses teaching students how to relax and deal with stress.
   c Should teenagers be able to leave school at 14? Write an article for a parenting magazine, discussing the pros and cons of this idea.
   d Are teenagers today better off than teenagers in the 1960s? Write a report on what teenagers' lives are like in the UK today.
   e Your headteacher wants to know your views about offering driving lessons in school time. Write a briefing paper for him on the subject.

2 Choose one of the tasks. Write a brief plan showing what features you would use in your writing for it.

Understanding style

You can work out from the purpose and audience of a writing task what style you should use.

If the task is:	Your style should be:	For example:
To write for an organisation – a business, local government office, school or charity. To write a legal or official document.	Formal standard English. Use correct grammar and no dialect words, slang, or contractions. Use sophisticated or technical vocabulary. Keep writing impersonal, using the third person.	The leisure facilities currently available are inadequate and council members must consider options for improvement carefully.
To write for an audience you know personally, and not in a legal, business or official context. To seem friendly and approachable, such as in an advert or blog.	Less formal standard English. Use correct grammar and no dialect or slang, but include a few contractions and informal phrases. Use everyday rather than technical vocabulary. Address the reader directly – you could use 'you' or 'I' statements, or questions.	The leisure facilities really aren't good enough and all of you in the community need to come up with some great ideas for how to improve them.

Activity 1

1 Read the tasks below, working out the purpose and audience for each.

2 Then decide on the style you should use for each of them.
   a Write a report for the Department for Children, Schools and Families on how toy advertising in November and December affects family life in the UK.
   b Write an article for a gap-year website discussing the pros and cons of taking a gap year and the best time to take one.
   c Write a leaflet for parents, explaining how to encourage teenagers to eat healthily.
   d Write an email to an older family friend or relative, explaining how they can make their home more secure.

3 Read these rough notes that Sam wrote for Task A.

> Kids pester parents from the minute ads for Christmas toys start on the TV. By November mums and dads have had enough! 'I want ... I want' and 'Everyone else is getting a...' = stress overload. Families in debt. Is that what DCSF wants?

4 Use Sam's notes to write a first draft for Task A in an appropriate style for the purpose and audience.

5 **a** Write a first draft of the opening paragraph for your response to Task C, taking care to suit your style to the audience and purpose.
   b Swap finished paragraphs with a partner. Decide whether they have written in the right style to suit the audience and purpose. Suggest any improvements they could make.
   c Redraft your own paragraph to take into account any suggestions your partner has made.

ResultsPlus
Top tip

Remember, your reader only has the words you have written to show them who you are and what you are trying to say. Unless you choose your words carefully, you may give the wrong impression and your meaning may not be clear.

This lesson will help you to:
▶ write a well-organised formal letter and email
▶ use paragraphs effectively
▶ ensure meaning is clear by using connectives effectively.

ResultsPlus
Top tip

The success of a formal letter depends a great deal on correct layout and organisation. You need to know where to place your address and the address of the person you are sending it to. You also need the date and the right form of greeting and closing salutation. If you are writing an email, your software automatically adds the date and your email address, but you should choose an appropriate greeting and closing salutation.

When you write a formal letter:
▶ Work out the best order for your points.
▶ Only include points that are relevant.
▶ Use the first paragraph to explain your purpose in writing.
▶ Use the last paragraph to make it clear what response you want.
▶ Set out the letter with your address and the recipient's address, the date, a greeting and a salutation.
▶ If you are writing to someone by name, end with the salutation 'Yours sincerely'.
▶ If you are writing to someone you don't know using 'Dear Sir' or 'Dear Madam', end with the salutation 'Yours faithfully'.
▶ Write in standard formal English.
▶ Use persuasive techniques if you need to.

Activity 1

1 a Study the letter opposite and one on page 73. Draw a diagram of how a formal letter should be laid out. Label the features with layout rules. Use the notes in the grid on pages 62–63 if you need help.
   b Study the email on page 80. How does it differ from a formal letter? List the rules you think you should follow when writing an email.

2 a Make a flowchart for the letter opposite, showing:
   • the main points the writer makes
   • the order of the points made.
   b How does the writer make sure his introduction and conclusion are effective?

3 a How has the writer made his letter appeal to his reader?
   b Which of the following persuasive features did he use in his letter?

persuasive vocabulary — adjectives, adverbs and vivid verbs
superlatives   emotive vocabulary
rhetorical questions   facts   opinions
reasons   ways of overcoming objections
appeal to reader's emotions
a vision of what the future could be like
anecdotes or stories

'Triffids'
32 Wyndham Terrace
Tynsham
Wiltshire

21st June 2010

Wilfred Torrence MP
House of Commons
London
SW1A 0AA

Dear Mr Torrence

I am writing to express my deep concern about the genetic engineering of animals and crops. We have no real understanding of the long-term impact of changing the genes in the plants and animals that make up our food. It is extremely dangerous to experiment without sufficient checks in place to make sure that we discover what long-term effect eating unnatural food will have on human beings. Surely we cannot just carry on feeding people genetically modified (GM) food until we discover that after ten or twenty years people suffer excruciating deadly diseases as a result?

Already GM crops such as soybeans, corn, canola and cotton seed oil are eaten by a huge number of people who may not even know they are taking such a risk. In the U.S., GM soybeans make up 89 per cent of all those eaten, and 60 per cent of corn and 75 per cent of rapeseed is GM. GM sugar cane and sugar beet, potatoes and rice have also been developed. Just think how much of people's diets may be GM. Does the government know or care how much GM food people in Britain are eating?

I know the idea of foods that are perfectly shaped, disease free and quick growing might seem wonderful. But is it really? If there is a long-term danger from any or all these foods, we are sitting on a ticking time bomb. The cost to the NHS could be immense. All because we are impatient and will not take the time to discover the real consequences but want to make as much money as possible from growing 'superfoods'.

I urge you, therefore, to vote against licensing further genetic engineering experiments involving food production and to stand against GM foods. The health of millions of families in the world depends on you taking this courageous action.

Yours sincerely

William Mason

Activity 2

1 You are now going to write your own formal letter. Read the following task, then work through the activities to complete it.

> Write a letter to the head teacher/principal of your school or college, persuading them that anytime access to online resources will benefit students' learning.

2 **a** First, come up with a list of ideas and examples to demonstrate how internet access can benefit students' learning.

b Then come up with a list of possible objections to your ideas, for example, cost. Work out how you could argue against each of those objections.

c Work out a list of reasons why the head teacher should act on your ideas. For example, using digital media will motivate students and make reading and writing more enjoyable and effective.

d How could you make your letter persuasive? Look at the list of persuasive features at the bottom of page 76. Work out examples of the different features that you could use in your letter.

3 Make a plan for your letter, using a chart like the one below.

Paragraph	Point	Supporting evidence, reasons etc.	Persuasive language
Introduction	Writing to suggest an effective way to boost students' motivation.	Using ICT is motivating Saves money spent on books, paper etc.	Rhetorical question, e.g. 'Would you like this school to achieve the best results in the country?' Appeal to desire to be the best.

4 Write a draft of your letter, making sure you set it out correctly.

5 Swap drafts with a partner. Read each other's letters.
- Check that your letters contain all the features listed on page 76.
- Find and tick the different persuasive techniques your partner has used. Use the grid on pages 62–63 to help you.

Paragraphs

Beginning a new paragraph when you write about a different time, place, event or idea helps your reader understand your text. Your paragraphs need to be well-organised so that they make sense. When you are writing any non-fiction text you can use the PEEL structure to help you.

Point – the first sentence in the paragraph tells readers its main point.

Evidence – next give readers facts and/or anecdotes to prove that the point is sensible.

Explore – after giving evidence, explore its significance. Explain the main point in more depth or add other smaller points related to it.

Link – end the paragraph by showing how it links to the main topic or the point in the next paragraph.

 Results**Plus**
Top tip

Effective use of paragraphs helps the reader by breaking up the text into smaller chunks of linked ideas and information on the same topic.

Use connectives to link your ideas **within** and **between** paragraphs. There is a list of useful ones on page 81.

Activity 1

1 a Re-read paragraph two of the formal letter on page 77. Work out how the PEEL structure is used.
  b Which of the paragraphs in the rest of the text use the PEEL structure?
  c Writers sometimes alter the order of the PEEL structure. Find two paragraphs that do not follow the PEEL structure and work out:
   • where the main point is made
   • where the evidence is given
   • where the exploration of the evidence is given.

Activity 2

1 Check your draft letter. Is it written in paragraphs? Where have you used the PEEL structure?

2 Study the paragraphs in a partner's draft. Make a note of how to improve three of them, for example, by adding evidence, or by sometimes beginning with the evidence rather than the point.

3 Using your partner's suggestions, re-draft your letter to improve your paragraphs.

Clear meaning – connectives

Connectives help you show how information and ideas link together in your writing — make sure you use the right one for the job. You can use a connective to:

▶ link ideas in a sentence

▶ link sentences in a paragraph

▶ link paragraphs together.

The table opposite shows how different connectives can be used.

Activity 1

1 Study the table opposite and make a table of your own like the one below, sorting the connectives into three groups.

A Those you know and often use in your writing	**B** Those you have heard of but do not use often or at all	**C** Those you do not know

2 In small groups, build up your knowledge by giving each other examples of how connectives can be used.

3 Read the email below. Which connectives has the writer used to link ideas:
  • inside sentences
  • between sentences
  • between paragraphs?

Delete   Reply   Reply All   Forward   Print

Dear Students

Although your suggestion for anytime internet access has great appeal, because funds are so limited we need to target our spending carefully. In addition, we need to ensure that the technology cannot be misused. Another concern is that we cannot afford a lot of training for staff.

Therefore, can you email me explaining how you would respond to these points and ensure that we can take your ideas on board successfully this year.

Best wishes

E Delve

4 Plan and write a reply to the email above. Give reasons for your views and use a range of connectives to link your points.

5 a Assess a partner's writing. Tick each connective your partner has used correctly, then count how many ticks they have.

b Try to increase the number and variety of connectives you use. Re-draft each other's emails using more from columns B and C of your table.

Connectives and link words	Use these to:
next then after that **later** **before** afterwards **while** meanwhile since **whenever** **when**	To tell readers what order events happen in. For example, 'Decide how you are going to get home. Then get ready to go.'
first **secondly** **thirdly** first of all **finally** to begin with **next** **in the first place**	To show readers which of your points are most important. For example, 'First of all make sure you know the time of the last bus home.'
also **too** in addition similarly **as** like even **another** **furthermore** **moreover**	To show the next point adds to the last point. These words are useful to persuade. For example, 'Not knowing how you'll get home is stupid, it also leaves you in danger.'
but **however** **although** though on the other hand **whereas** **in contrast** nonetheless besides	To show the next point goes against the last one you made. These link words are useful to argue. For example, 'Although most people are good people, on the other hand you can't be sure that someone you've just met at a club is a safe person to take you home.'
because **therefore** **so** then **for example** for instance also **similarly** **another**	To explain. 'For example, you might be safer sharing a taxi back because it will drop you off at your home so that you don't have to walk back alone from the bus stop.'
then because **but** **however** **also** **similarly** for example for instance	When writing a review,. For example, 'If you're choosing a club for its safety points then Electric has lots to offer, for example the bouncers call taxis for you.'
because **since** but **therefore** **however** **another** **similarly** notwithstanding	In an argument. For example, 'Since drugs are illegal, clubs should make sure they are not being sold on their premises. Notwithstanding this, clubs often turn a blind eye, which means it is up to you to resist the temptation. Therefore this makes it harder for ex-addicts to stay clean if they go out clubbing with their mates.'
on the one hand...on the other hand... in the same way **alternatively**	To balance points against each other. For example, 'On the one hand women should be free to wear what they like, on the other hand are they making themselves vulnerable if their clothes are too revealing?'

6 Planning and organising your writing

The key to presenting complex information clearly is to spend time planning your writing carefully. You need a clear idea of:

- your audience and purpose and the form and style you need to use
- what information you need to include
- how to present the information clearly
- how to avoid repeating yourself
- how to be concise.

Results Plus
Top tip

Read the task carefully to help you decide on the main points you are going to include. Think about how you will lay out your article to make it easy to read and attractive.

Activity 1

1 Read the task below carefully.

> Write a 500-word magazine article for young adult readers on getting a job.
>
> You may like to include instructions and advice on finding out about jobs that will suit the readers, getting the right qualifications, writing a CV and letter of application, and interview techniques.

2 Note down:
   a Who your audience is and what they need to know.
   b What your purpose is and what you need to include to achieve it.
   c What form you must write in.
   d What style will suit your purpose and audience.

   Look at pages 62–63 for help if you need to.

3 Now you can plan your writing.
   a First, note down what you should include. Make a spider diagram plan.
   - Write the main idea of the task in a circle in the middle of a blank piece of paper.
   - Using the suggestions made in the task, and your own ideas, add a 'leg' to the circle for each area you need to write about. Remember to include an introduction and a conclusion.
   - Add further ideas and points to each leg.
   Use the example below to get you started.

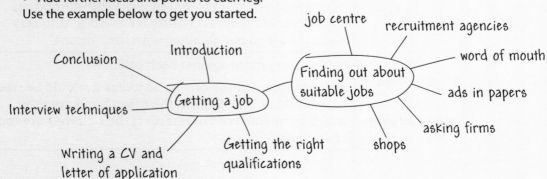

b Now work out a sensible order for the different points. Number the points on your spider diagram plan like the example below.

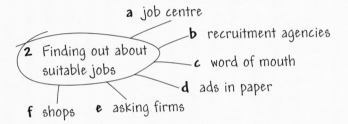

a job centre

b recruitment agencies

2 Finding out about suitable jobs

c word of mouth

d ads in paper

f shops   e asking firms

4 Turn your plan into a series of paragraph plans like the one below. You could use the chart on page 81 to help you to link points.

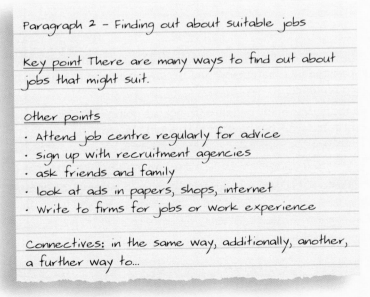

Paragraph 2 – Finding out about suitable jobs

<u>Key point</u> There are many ways to find out about jobs that might suit.

<u>Other points</u>
· Attend job centre regularly for advice
· sign up with recruitment agencies
· ask friends and family
· look at ads in papers, shops, internet
· Write to firms for jobs or work experience

<u>Connectives:</u> in the same way, additionally, another, a further way to...

5 Write a first draft of your magazine article. Use your plan to make sure you organise your points clearly.

Clear meaning – subject-verb agreement

After writing, you should always check your draft. Make sure that the meaning of every sentence is clear. When you read each sentence, make sure the subject and verb agree. The verbs must be right for the number of people doing the action. To check this:

▶ find the verb, for example 'is working', 'are applying'.

▶ decide who or what is doing the verb – they are known as the **agent**.

▶ check that the verb is written in the right way for that number of agents.

> ✔ He is hoping to be given work experience.
> ✗ He are hoping to be given work experience.

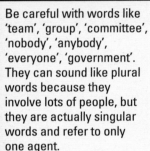

ResultsPlus
Watch out!

Be careful with words like 'team', 'group', 'committee', 'nobody', 'anybody', 'everyone', 'government'. They can sound like plural words because they involve lots of people, but they are actually singular words and refer to only one agent.
✔ The <u>team</u> **is** working on a project.
Remember also that if two singular agents are doing one action, the verb needs to be plural.
✔ <u>Volunteering</u> and <u>doing work experience</u> **are** good ways to find out about whether a job is suitable.

Activity 1

1 a For each of the sentences below, work out how many agents are carrying out the underlined verb. Then decide whether the form of the verb is correct for that number of agents.

b Rewrite any sentences whose number of agents and verb form do not match.

  A If a person <u>want</u> to find out what qualifications you need for a job, look at www.careersadvice.direct.gov.uk.

  B There are podcasts where people <u>explain</u> what it is like to do their job.

  C Answering the career values questionnaire <u>help</u> people work out what sort of job to do.

  D There's even a forum where site visitors <u>chats</u> about different issues.

  E The site also <u>explains</u> how to gain any qualifications you need.

Activity 2

1 Read the student's draft below, and decide what the missing verb is in each sentence.

2 Think about how many people or things are doing the action in each sentence, and work out how the verb should be written.

> _____ to a careers adviser to find out what sort of job would suit your personality and interests. An adviser can also tell you what qualifications you _____. Amy _____ to be a police officer, and was given lots of information. Whatever job you _____, a good site to use _____ careersadvice.direct.gov.uk.

Activity 3

Dan writes an informal blog on finding a job, and wants to use one of his entries for the magazine article. He needs to check his work and improve its accuracy. Help him by finding and correcting the six errors in subject-verb agreement.

For anyone in an area of high unemployment, searching for a job can seem hopeless. However, try to keep a positive attitude. After all, some people has got jobs and someone will get the new jobs that comes along – and that someone could be you. Everyone know you should be doing all you can to make your CV stand out. Think about what will make yours looks better. Is it worth going back to college to get new qualifcations? Should you look at another area of work? Volunteering and trying to get work experience is good ways to learn new skills and shows you are doing something useful with your time.

In the long term, it may be worth considering moving to an area of higher employment, or to start with you may need to take a slightly different job from the one you would ideally like. If you take that less than ideal job at least you are working and you is going to be able to try moving across to your ideal job later on.

Activity 4

Go back to the draft text of your magazine article.

1 Read a partner's text and discuss:
   • any ways in which the ideas or information in the text can be made clearer
   • how to improve any sentences where meaning is unclear
   • any verbs that you think may be wrong.

2 Correct and improve your draft using the feedback your partner has given you.

This lesson will help you to:
- research and write a briefing paper
- make meaning clear by using apostrophes correctly.

Briefing papers are used to give information on particular subjects, and suggest possible courses of action. When writing a briefing paper, remember:

- You are writing for a particular audience. Ask yourself what they already understand, and what they need to know.
- State who the paper is for at the top left of your page.
- Give your paper a title that makes its purpose clear.
- Organise the information under these four headings:
  - **Issue:** state what the briefing paper is about and why your audience needs to read it.
  - **Background:** give information, history and explanations that will help your reader to consider the issues.
  - **Considerations:** list options, with pros and cons and analysis.
  - **Conclusion:** pinpoint in a few sentences what the current situation is and state what you think should happen next – your recommendations.
- Use different ways of presenting information – normal text, headings, bullet lists, numbered lists, etc. – to help readers find the information they need.
- Write in standard English.

Activity 1

1 a Read the briefing paper opposite. It was written for Philip Goodman, the product developer of Goodall Clothing.
  b Consider how each feature is used and decide how it helps Philip to understand the issue. For example, ' Giving him the pros and cons of … helps him understand…'.

2 Based on the information in the briefing paper, could Philip make a decision about what action he needs to take? Give reasons for your answer.

Goodall Clothing

Briefing paper for Product Developer: Philip Goodman

Increasing the appeal of our clothing to children aged 6–12

Issue
To find new and increased markets for Goodall Clothing's products by meeting current trends and providing value for money.

Background
Goodall Clothing targets lower-income families. As children grow older they have more say in what they wear; this means that clothes for the 6–12 sector must have real child appeal. Our current best-selling range for older girls relies on the popularity of Cheryl Cole's style, without using her name or image.

Considerations
Options
- using real characters and personality tie-ins from TV and films
- creating more character brands mirroring current favourites.

Pros
- children's passion for the person is transferred to the clothes: they want to buy the clothes to be like their hero
- creating more mirror brands gives our products wider appeal.

Cons
- cost – paying for tie-ins drives up the cost of our clothes
- children who dislike a character won't buy the clothes
- risk – if a person's popularity suddenly falls we will be left with clothes we can't sell.

Analysis
We need to consider whether the benefits are greater than the costs and risk.

Conclusion/recommendations
The brand based on Cheryl Cole's style is selling well. We should investigate the cost of using her name/image to increase sales further, as well as developing new mirror brands to spread the risk.

Activity 2

1 Read the task below and note the key words that tell you who you are
writing for and what information your notes must include. Think about what
your audience might already know, and what they will need to find out.

2 Write a briefing paper for your head teacher and governors. They need
to know how to help your school or college to be more environmentally
friendly by reducing car use, cutting energy bills, improving recycling, etc.

3 Start to write your briefing paper, following the layout of the example on
page 87:

   a State who your paper is for.

   b Work out a title that tells the reader the purpose of the briefing.

   c Under the subheading 'Issue', sum up what your briefing paper is about
and why your audience needs to read it.

   d Under the subheading 'Background', make notes on:
- the current situation
- the history
- any explanation that is needed.

   e Write the subheading 'Considerations' and list under it:
- the options for what might be done
- the pros and cons of each of the options.

   f Add any analysis under a separate heading.

   g Finally, write a conclusion. State in a few sentences what the current
situation is and what you think should happen next.

Apostrophes

You need to use punctuate accurately to make sure your briefing notes are clear. This involves using apostrophes correctly.

An apostrophe can show where letters are missing from a word. It goes where the missing letters should be.

> It is ⇨ It's
> Could not ⇨ couldn't

An apostrophe can make it clear who an object belongs to, and how many people own it.

▶ Place an apostrophe before an 's' if it is a single owner.

> The boy's shirt

▶ Place an apostrophe after an 's' if it there is more than one owner.

> The boys' shirt

When you check your writing, always work out what the apostrophes are telling your reader about how many people own each thing, or where letters have been left out.

Activity 1

1 a Study where each apostrophe is placed in the sentence below. Work out whether one or many boys, schools and lab technicians are being talked about.

The boys' red football shirts were dumped in the school's washing machine. They stained the lab technician's white lab-coats pink.

b Rewrite the sentence above, moving the apostrophes to change the numbers of boys and lab technicians.

2 In the sentence below, the writer has missed out apostrophes while contracting words. Write the sentence again, this time putting apostrophes in the correct places.

If students dont have checklists they cant revise how to write each form.

3 Read a partner's briefing papers and check their use of apostrophes:
- Tick (✓) apostrophes that are correctly used to show possession.
- Star (*) any apostrophes that are correctly used to show where letters are missing.
- <u>Underline</u> any words where an apostrophe has been missed out or needs correcting. Write **C** in the margin if the apostrophe is needed for contraction, and **P** if it is needed for possession.

4 Write a final draft of your briefing paper, making sure you use apostrophes correctly.

To present your argument convincingly, you need to plan the points you will make and how you will back them up with evidence. Consider what evidence you have and how you can use it to support your point of view. How will you put your points together to build a convincing argument? Try to think of arguments against your point of view that you may need to overcome.

Activity 1

1 Read the task below carefully.

> Write a magazine article in which you argue **either** for **or** against the idea that too much advertising is harmful.

2 First, decide what your purpose and audience are, and what form and style you must write in. Find an example of the correct form and make a checklist of features to include.

3 Now start to plan your argument. Think about the advantages and disadvantages of advertising. Note your ideas in two lists like the examples opposite. Decide which viewpoint you will take.

4 **a** Think of evidence and examples to back up the points you want to make.
   b Next, study the points for the opposite viewpoint to the one you have chosen. Work out an argument against each of them. Jot down any evidence or examples you can use, for example:

> Point: Small businesses that advertise are able to compete with big businesses.

> Argument against it: Small businesses can't afford the same level of advertising as big businesses.

> Evidence: A small local café doesn't have the same advertising budget as a global chain like Starbucks.

ResultsPlus
Top tip

Your writing will have more impact if you can back up and develop the points you make. Check the information you have been given in the task to guide you how to do this. For example, think about what kind of evidence might be effective in convincing your audience of your argument.

5 Work out the best order for your points. Decide which ones are similar and draw lines to link them together: presenting them together will help to build your argument. Number the points in the order you decide on.

Arguments for why advertising is harmful:
- Ads are everywhere – no one can get any peace
- Ads make people unhappy if they can't afford things
- Ads make things sound better than they are – so people are disappointed
- People compare themselves with 'perfect' models in ads – can lead to eating disorders
- Ads make people's possessions seem too important and don't value e.g. relationships
- Children believe what they see in adverts
- Ads make children greedy
- Ads promote unhealthy things, e.g. junk food
- Ads are bad for small businesses that can't afford to advertise on the same scale as bigger businesses

Arguments for why advertising is not harmful and can be helpful:
- Ads are a way of earning money for good things, e.g. sport
- You can choose not to view them, e.g. turn off TV ads
- Ads give people choices
- Advertising forces businesses to compete on price, value, etc.
- Ads cause less harm than e.g. newspapers and magazines that write about people in a way that is upsetting for them and create gossip about celebrities
- Ads create jobs – for advertisers and in companies making products
- Advertising of health advice, charity information etc. can save or improve lives
- There are restrictions on some harmful advertising, e.g. fast food for kids, alcohol
- Advertising helps small businesses to compete with big ones.

A PEEL plan can help you to build your argument. (You can remind yourself of how a PEEL plan works by reading page 79.) For example:

Point – ads are everywhere
Evidence – on TV and radio at least every 15 minutes, newspapers, mags, billboards, trains etc.
Explain why the evidence supports your point of view – can't escape ads or make a decision without being affected by them. Make people dissatisfied.
Link the point to the question or the next point – not as simple as switching off the TV...

Activity 2

1 Make a PEEL paragraph plan like the one on page 91 for each of your points.

Make sure you grab your readers' attention. Think of a catchy heading and an interesting introduction. You could use a question, an anecdote or a statement. For example:

Question: 'Do small children understand that adverts show an imaginary world?'

Anecdote: 'My younger brother believes everything adverts tell him. He thinks buying a Ben 10 outfit will make him a hero.'

Statement: 'Children do not understand that adverts are not real.'

Vary the way you begin each paragraph. For example, you could state your point, or start with a piece of evidence.

Finally, make sure your conclusion is powerful and memorable – perhaps ask a thought-provoking question, for example: 'Do you really want the advertisers to run your life for you?'

Activity 3

Go back to your plan and make sure you have ideas for a good heading, introduction and conclusion. Plan to vary how you introduce each point in a new paragraph.

Clear meaning – inverted commas

You can use inverted commas to show your reader three things:

1 That the words inside the inverted commas are a quotation of what someone has said, or a piece of text from somewhere else, for example:

> The controller of BBC1 stated that 'Adverts will never appear on the BBC.'

2 That the words inside the inverted commas are the title of a book, song, newspaper, play, poem, television programme or film.

> An advert is as real to a small child as 'Dora the Explorer' or 'Ben 10'.

3 That you know the word or phrase is slang, or being used in a special way.

> It might seem 'uncool' to care about advertising for children.

1 Molly has drafted part of her article, and now needs to go back and check her use of inverted commas. Copy the following extract from her work and correct the inverted commas in at least eight places.

> Without advertising there would be no money to make my favourite programmes and show them on prime-time television. But more than that, I would miss the ads themselves. I don't care if that makes me a 'loser. I enjoyed Talk Talk boasting about being a brighter brand. It breaks up the over-excitement of X Factor watching all those crazy people light-dancing. I like watching the manic gorilla drumming 'In The Air Tonight as he persuades me to eat chocolate. I like chorusing because we're worth it with Cheryl Cole and If we save today we can save tomorrow on the energy ad. I even look forward to seeing what Kris Marshall is being forced to do in the next instalment in the long-running BT ad-story. Perhaps I'd learn more reading serious articles in The Times, but would I have as much fun?
>
> Without advertising there would be no football in this country, the Olympics couldn't function and thousands of young men and women would never achieve their sporting dreams, says Anna Fritz, Chief Exeutive of Sponsor Me. She is right: the contribution made by advertising sponsorship to sport is huge.

2 a Now write your magazine article or blog, using your plan. Make sure you use inverted commas correctly.
 b When you have finished, swap texts with a partner and check each other's work.
 • Is the writing appropriate to its audience and purpose and written in the correct form and style?
 • Is the viewpoint well argued?
 • Check the inverted commas: tick each place where your partner has used them correctly and put a cross to show where they have been missed out or used wrongly.

This lesson will help you to:
▶ write a report
▶ use verbs in correct tenses so that meaning is clear
▶ ensure meaning is clear by improving your spelling
▶ check your work to ensure it is clear and accurate.

ResultsPlus
Top tip

Don't confuse this kind of report – the presentation of factual evidence about a subject aiming to produce one or more conclusions and recommendations for action – with a news report.

When you write a report:

▶ Include a heading that makes the purpose of the report clear.
▶ Organise the information you want your reader to know so that it is easy to find.
▶ Use headings, bullet lists, numbered lists and different type styles such as bold or italics to help readers find the information they need.
▶ Tell readers why the report is being written in the introduction.
▶ Use the main part of the report to explain what evidence was gathered and what you think it means.
▶ Sum up your findings in a conclusion, and then make recommendations.
▶ Include facts and figures as evidence.
▶ Write in formal standard English.

Activity 1

1 Read the report opposite. How has the writer made the information clear by using the features listed above?

2 **a** Find the main points in the report.
   b Make a flow chart showing the order in which they are given.

3 **a** Compare the evidence used with the recommendations. Work out which facts the writer used to support each recommendation.
   b What other recommendations could you make, based on this evidence?

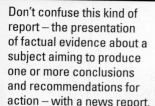

Conserving energy at Chilton's Outdoor Activities Centre

Although there is a 25 per cent difference between our winter and summer energy bills, because we do not heat our offices, public rooms and bedrooms from May to September, energy bills remain high. If we can reduce energy bills by cutting waste, then more funds will become available to improve the environment for staff and guests in other ways. This report looks at how and why energy is wasted in the centre and recommends ways to avoid this.

The most likely causes of energy waste

The main areas of energy use in the centre are heating, water heating, equipment, laundry and food storage and cooking. Excessive energy loss for each of these areas resulted from:

- setting thermostats for central and water heating higher than necessary
- poor insulation of doors and windows
- leaving appliances on standby when they are not in use
- using old machines that are not energy efficient
- using high-energy light bulbs, and leaving lights on in unoccupied rooms
- washing guests' towels, sheets etc. at over-hot temperatures and drying them in the tumble dryer
- setting fridge freezer thermostats too low
- cooking with ovens rather than microwaves or hobs.

The reasons for energy waste

Energy is often wasted because people are unaware of the energy cost of their actions. *For example, one person unloading the frozen food delivery uses more energy than several people doing it at the same time and opening the freezer store only once for a shorter period.*

People are unaware of how energy loss adds up over time. *For example, if every day a high-energy light bulb is left on for 10 minutes when it is not needed, that adds up to 2.5 days' unnecessary use per year.*

The centre has been reluctant to spend money replacing old equipment that is still working. *For example there is an old fridge in the kitchen which has a D energy rating; it could be replaced with a new model that has rating A.*

Conclusion

It is clear that simple measures can be taken to address energy waste. Recommendations for action are given below.

1 Thermostats should be adjusted.
2 The cost of better insulation should be investigated.
3 Equipment should be gradually replaced by more efficient models, and in the meantime should not be left on standby.
4 Lightbulbs should be changed to low-energy ones.
5 Energy-efficient cooking and food-storing methods should be used.
6 Laundry should be line-dried when possible.
7 Staff should be trained in energy efficiency.
8 Posters should encourage guests and staff to save energy.

Activity 2

Write a report on how your school or home could save energy. This will be read by the people with responsibility for managing the budget and paying the bills.

1 Make a list of all the different ways energy is used in your school or home. For example, lighting, heating, cooking, computers, tools. You can use ideas from the report on page 95 to help you.

2 Use your list to investigate how things could be improved. Record your findings in a table like the one below.

Energy use	Current situation	Possible improvements
Lighting – bulbs	No low-energy bulbs. Lights are often left on in empty rooms.	Change all to low-energy bulbs and teach people to turn off lights in unused rooms.

3 Based on your findings, make a list of things you would recommend changing and why.

4 Plan your report. Use a planning frame like the one below to help you organise your information.

Sections	Information
Introduction What is the report about?	To find out how Barton College could become more energy efficient and make recommendations.
Main evidence Organise your evidence into sections with headings.	Section 1: Evidence about light energy. Section 2: Evidence about heat energy.
What the evidence shows	A lot of energy could be saved by...
Recommendations	Use words like 'should', 'might', 'could' to list your recommendations.

5 Use your plan to write a first draft of your report. Use the checklist of features of reports on page 94 to help you.

Verb tenses

You need to use verbs accurately to make sure your report is clear.

▶ Verbs (action and event words in a sentence) must refer correctly to the time when things happen – the past, present or future.

Past tense	Present tense	Future tense
I switched off the lights.	I switch off the lights.	I will switch off the lights.

▶ Some words signal the verb tense you need to write in. For example, '**In the future**, Barton College will buy A-rated energy-efficient appliances'.

▶ When you are writing about the same event or group of events, make sure you keep to a single tense.

Activity 1

1 Sunita has made notes for a paragraph of her report. What changes should she make for her final draft so that it is all in the present tense?

> At the moment we are wasting a lot of energy in my home. We had normal light bulbs in every light socket and we left them on all the time. No one remembers to turn the television off when they go out of the room either. The television and computer were left on standby all night. The energy ratings of the fridge, washing machine and oven were all D.

2 Sarah jotted down her ideas for the task and now needs to write a final draft. Which verbs does she need to change so that it is all in the present tense?

> In my school we have been trying to save energy for some time. We have stickers up reminding people to turn off lights but most people forgot. To save energy, we do not have hand dryers but the paper towels made a real mess everywhere. The ovens, fridges, dishwashers etc are all A energy rating which was good. Most of the computers and photocopiers will power down if they are not used for a while. We have the windows open a lot so heat went out of the classrooms but at least it is not stuffy.

3 **a** Read a partner's report and check the use of verbs.
   - Tick verbs that are in the same tense throughout a paragraph.
   - Underline any verbs that mark a change to a different tense.
   - In the recommendations, put a star by verbs in the future tense.
   b Redraft your report, correcting any verbs that are in the wrong tense.

Spelling

Whenever you write a text you need to make sure your spelling is accurate so that your reader will understand your meaning. You already know how to spell a lot of words correctly and use different ways to help you remember the spellings of words you find difficult. Now build on this and explore which strategies work best for you.

Learn to spell a new word

What has helped you before when learning the spelling of a new word? Ask your friends for tips.

> I look it up in the dictionary then write it out ten times.

> I use Look, Cover, Say, Write.

> I use a rhyme or message, for example 'Necessary – a shirt with one collar and two sleeves.'

> I highlight the part of the word that's tricky.

Tricky parts of words

If you sometimes spell part of a word incorrectly, find a way to help yourself remember it. For example, 'infinite has a nit in it'.

Homophones

Homophones are words that sound the same but are spelt differently, such as their/there/they're. Make up rules to help you remember which one to use, for example:

▶ When I can ask 'where', I need to write 'there'.

▶ If it belongs to someone, I need to write 'their'.

▶ If the word is short for they are, I need to write 'they're'.

Activity 2

1 Read through your report and underline any words you are unsure that you spelled correctly.
   a Use a dictionary to check the spelling of each one and write it out correctly.
   b Choose one of the learning strategies listed above and learn to spell each word.
   c Work with a partner and test each other.

2 Which homophones do you sometimes get wrong? Work out a rule to help you remember how and when to use them, then check your report to see if you used them correctly. Correct any mistakes.

Checking your work

Use this list to help you check any text you are working on for accuracy.

▶ Has it got all the features you would expect in the text type?

▶ Do your language, content and presentation suit your readers?

▶ Will it achieve its purpose?

▶ Have you included the right content?

▶ Is it formal or informal enough all the way through?

▶ Does each sentence make sense? Read the text 'aloud' in your head to check.

▶ Check for homophones – have you used the right one?

▶ Read the text backwards, focusing on the spelling of each word. Correct any errors

ResultsPlus
Top tip

Try to leave some time to proofread your work carefully. Check that:
• it reads correctly
• the punctuation makes your meaning clear
• your spelling is accurate, especially that of everyday words and the words given to you in the question.
Rewrite any parts that need to be improved.

Activity 3

1 Practise using the checklist above to find ways to improve the final draft of a text.
  a Check the draft below and suggest ten ways of improving it.
  b Compare your ideas with a partner's. Together, re-write the text, making the improvements you agree are needed.

> In the future we should give people reward points for saving energy eg for turning of lights when they leaves there classrooms. That wold make people want too do it. They're should be a ruler that everytime we bought a knew machine it had to be A rated for Energy.

2 a Now use the checklist to check your own report carefully.
  b Swap reports with a partner and check each other's. Use different colours to circle any errors that you missed or spotted which your partner did not.

3 a Make a list of the errors you made in your report. Then find and learn the rules that will help you to avoid making them again.
  b Set yourself the goal of trying not to make three of your mistakes again. Write it at the top of your next draft of the report like this:

> In my report I will:
> • spell there/their/they're correctly
> • use the future tense for all my recommendations
> • make sure I use paragraphs to organise my information.

Activity 4

Write a final draft of your report, trying to get right the things you just learnt.

Afterwards, check it carefully and mark in any changes needed. Did you achieve your target?

Writing mini-test – questions

On these pages you will find examples of the kinds of tasks you may encounter in your Writing test. For these practice tasks, you have been given some tips by the examiner. Use these to develop your skills – but remember, you won't be given these tips in the test.

Task 1

Information

Your local newspaper is holding a competition to win a free day out. To enter the competition you must write an article with the title, 'Best of British – three top ideas for a cheap day out for all the family without leaving the country'. The paper has given you these ideas to get you started.

Best of British

Fabulous country and seaside destinations such as Cornwall or the Lake District. Beautiful walks, stunning scenery, a wealth of affordable accommodation.

Exciting cities, with world-class theatres, restaurants, museums and shopping.

Stay-cations in your own area – explore the walks, cycle paths, parks, leisure facilities and picnic spots close to home for no-cost days out.

Thrilling theme parks, farms, zoos and activity centres with something for everyone.

Writing task

Write an article for the newspaper in which you suggest three ideas for affordable family days out in the UK. In your article you may include:
- information about your suggestions
- reasons for your suggestions
- information about cost, including travel and accommodation if necessary.

(15 marks)

ResultsPlus
Top tip

Plan your answer before you start to write. You have to give **three** ideas for a **day out** that **does not cost very much** for **all the family**. Make sure you are clear about why you are writing the article (your purpose) and who are you writing it for (your audience).

Decide on how to organise your material. Plan to use sub-headings to separate different sections, and use paragraphs and bullet-points to make your article easy to read. Do not try to write in columns.

Choose your words carefully and use a variety of sentence structures. Proof read your work very carefully. At least 40% of the marks overall for Writing are awarded for technical accuracy, so check your spelling, punctuation and grammar carefully.

Task 2

Information

You have booked through a travel agency, Nationwide Travel, two advance train tickets for yourself and a friend to go to Edinburgh on holiday. When the tickets arrive they are accompanied by this letter.

Nationwide Travel

Nationwide Travel
Fuller Street
Myhill-on-Sea
MY7 1FX

Dear Customer,

I am pleased to enclose two standard class tickets from your local station to Edinburgh, as requested.

Please note, however, that since your booking the timetable for this service has been updated. This means that you will now be travelling on June 10th instead of June 11th, and your train will leave at 6am rather than 10am. The cost remains the same as at time of booking.

Yours sincerely

Gary Oliver
Manager

Writing task

Write a letter to the manager of Nationwide Travel to complain about the change of travel arrangements and request new tickets at a time and date more convenient to you.

(10 marks)

ResultsPlus
Top tip

Make sure you understand the context for your writing before you begin. Read carefully both the 'Information' section and the writing task itself.

Present the letter in the right form and use paragraphs to make it as clear as possible. Make sure your paragraphs follow a logical order.

Be formal and polite in the way you express yourself, even though you may be annoyed. Write in standard English. Remember, you will gain marks for using language effectively and appropriately for the task. Finally, check your work carefully to make sure you have used correct spelling, punctuation and grammar.

On pages 102–105 you will find two example 'pass' answers to task 1 from page 100. On pages 106–109 are two example 'fail' answers to the same task. Read the answers together with the examiner comments to help you understand what is required to achieve a Level 2 pass.

Student 1 – extracts typical of 'pass Level 2' answers

Three top ideas for a cheap day out for all the family

The first top idea for a family day out would be to go out to a lovely local zoo, this is very helpful and also very fun and your kids get to learn a bit about Animals aswell. I can remember when I went to the zoo for the first time, it was amazing. I thought that it was the best time of my life seeing all the Animals and eating lovely chocolate! The zoo costs are relatively low and it is a fun day for the whole family to enjoy.

The second top idea for a cheap and great day out is to go to the park, a wonderful place to go and see all the trees and grass swaying in the wind. You can relax and let the kids go and kick around a football and run free, while you lie down and enjoy the warm sun. Taking the kids to the park is brilliant and all you take with you is a lovely Lunch! You may also have some spare time to teach the kids about different birds and wildlife.

The third top idea would be to take your family to the museum. This allows a great range of education and a fun day out. There is usually a lunch area where you can sit down and relax to eat if you get hungary looking at all those statues!

Examiner summary

What has been done well?	
The answer fits the task	Clear description of three suggestions for a cheap day out for all the family. Reasons given and some focus on cost.
Appropriate for the purpose	Task is fairly formal, but quite light-hearted. Some informality is acceptable, such as use of direct address, 'you can relax…'
Clear structure	Clear heading and new paragraph for each suggestion. Underlining 'first' etc helps the reader to follow the text.
Mostly accurate spelling	Most words are correct.
Some accurate punctuation	Full stops and exclamation marks used correctly.
Mostly correct grammar	Accurate subject-verb agreement and use of tenses.

What could be improved?	
Too much use of the first person 'I'	Suggestions should appeal to everyone and not be too personal. More varied language needed.
More direct information about cost	Actual details of costs would be better.
Be more specific	For example, give names of local zoos, parks and museums, and directions for getting there.
Improve use of commas	Sentences are sometimes not properly separated. In the first sentence, the comma should be a full stop followed by a new sentence beginning with 'This is very helpful…'
Use capital letters only where necessary	'Animals' in paragraph 1 and 'Lunch' in paragraph 2 should not begin with capital letters.

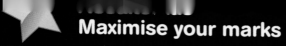

Student 2 – extracts typical of 'pass Level 2' answers

Eleanor Smith
Flat 4, DickensHouse
Park Street
London
SW1 4HB

Nationwide Travel
Fuller Street
Myhill-on-Sea
MY7 1FX

Dear Sir/Madam

I am writing to complain about the train tickets I booked to Edinburgh Ref. No: EDI5929.

When I booked the tickets through your South-West London branch, your staff were unhelpful and did not seem to understand my requests. The staff said that they would post the tickets to my home address.

When the tickets arrived, the date printed on the Intercity train from London to Edinburgh was June 10th, not June 11th as I requested. The time was also different. The letter explained that this was due to a change in service, but the staff had not contacted me to check if the new date and time were convenient.

I would like you to arrange new tickets at for a date and time when we are able to travel. I would also expect some reduction in the cost to compensation me for the inconvenience. I am very disappointed and want this issue to be resolved in time for my holiday.

To conclude, I am disgusted with your efforts and hope never to use Nationwide Travel again.

Yours faithfully

Eleanor Smith

Examiner summary

What has been done well?	
Answer fits the task	Correct form used and all relevant points included.
Mostly correct layout for a formal letter	Addresses set out properly, and salutation and sign off included.
Clear explanation of complaint and action expected. Relevant details included.	Details from task given, plus additional details such as a booking reference.
Tone is correct	Clear and business-like language. Formal vocabulary and no slang.
Accurate spelling	No spelling mistakes. Student has copied details from the question correctly.
Accurate punctuation	Full stops and commas used correctly.
Correct grammar	Accurate subject-verb agreement and use of tenses. Sentences varied and correct.

What could be improved?	
Some errors in format	Sender's name should not be included before the address.
Small error in content	Recipient's name was given – Gary Oliver – so should be used.
Date should be included	Always date formal letters so you can refer to them easily in future discussions.

Student 3 – extracts typical of 'fail Level 2' answers

One of the most expensive family days out and what is no doubtly one of the most inspiring days out you would ever have with your family would have to be the middle fields. You have archery, canoeing, absailing, rockclimbing, scubadiving, bungeejumping and adventure coarse. When you have done your day of adventure you can relax in a 5 star hotel where you get a heated swimming pool, 3 jacusese, a spa, games room including pool, table tennis, snooker and darts, a arcade room, a outside rollercoaster and a pub with wi fi skysports and BBC1, 2 and 3. It is lovly and it is quickly riseing to be one of the best family attractions for the decade so get yourself and your family booked now before its to late

Examiner summary

What has been done well?	
Logical organisation of information	All activities grouped together followed by list of leisure facilities for relaxation.
Clear description of some attractive details	List of activities and facilities available.
Good expression of ideas	Complex sentences have been used.
Some accurate spelling	Correct spelling of some difficult words – 'adventure', 'inspiring'
Some accurate punctuation	Commas used correctly in list.

What could be improved?	
Answer does not fit the task	Student has not read the task carefully enough so has only included one expensive suggestion instead of three cheap ones.
Structure needs more work	Heading needed to give subject of article. Paragraphs grouping ideas would help the reader to follow the information.
Information is not developed	Information needed on activities suitable for a family, and on cost.
Some errors in spelling	Words which sound the same sometimes mean different things – e.g. coarse/course, to/too. Student has made errors in this, as well as other spelling mistakes. Careful checking needed.
Some errors in punctuation	Apostrophe and full stop missing from last line.
Check grammar	First long sentence needs commas to separate ideas. Start proper names with capitals, e.g. Middle Fields

Student 4 – extracts typical of 'fail Level 2' answers

47 gutters end,

London Se8

2Se

Nationwide Travel

Fuller Street

Myhill-on-Sea

MY7 IFX

Dear Mr.dagger

I would like to inform you that the date on my tickets is not suitable and would like to replace the error with the correct date, as I have only a few weeks left until my flight. I would like the incident sorted as fast as possible please. please inform me if there are any further changes.

Sincerely, Israel Jones

Examiner summary

What has been done well?	
Partly correct format and layout	Addresses given in the right places. Greeting and sign off used.
Correct tone	Writing is formal and polite.
Some accuracy	No spelling mistakes and punctuation mostly correct. Address from task has been copied correctly.

What could be improved?	
Answer does not fit the task	Tickets were for a rail journey not a flight. Name of addressee is wrong.
Layout and format need more work	Addresses not laid out correctly, signature should be on separate line. Date needed.
Information lacks details	Need to state date and time of travel wanted, how many tickets, etc
State clearly what action is required	Too vague to say incident should be 'sorted'.
Check punctuation	Final sentence should be split with a full stop after first 'please'.
Check accuracy	Capitals needed for names and places.

Introduction to Functional Skills English Assessment

This section of the book will help you to prepare for your Functional Skills English Level 2 assessment.

Understand how you will be assessed

You will be assessed for your skills in:

▶ Reading

▶ Speaking, listening and communication

▶ Writing

On the following pages you will find a description of exactly how you will be assessed for each area, plus top tips from the examiner on how to gain as many marks as possible in each of your assessments. These tips are based on the examiner's experience of marking Functional Skills English assessments. Use them to prepare to make sure you secure every mark that you can.

Practice assessments

You will then be given practice exams and assessments:

▶ Pages 116–24 – practice Reading paper

▶ Pages 125–126 – practice Speaking, Listening and Communication assessment tasks

▶ Pages 127–28 – practice Writing paper

ResultsPlus
Self-assessment

When you have completed the assessments, review your work with a partner or with your teacher. Look at the 'top tips' from the examiner. What areas of your work are you confident in and what needs further improvement? Record your self-assessment, and set a plan for any areas you need to work on.

Your reading is assessed in one 45-minute exam. The total number of marks for the reading paper is 25.

The reading paper is divided into three sections, A, B and C. Each section has a text to read and questions to answer about it. Each question states the number of marks it is worth. All three texts are on the same subject or theme. You will be given space to write your answers.

The table below shows the types of question you will be asked and what you should do in each case.

Types of question	What you should do
Identify the main purpose of the text	Give a short written answer.
Multiple choice	Select the correct option to complete an unfinished sentence or to answer a question. Put a cross in a box to show your answer.
Find a number of pieces of information and evidence in the text	Give short written answers.
Decide whether statements you are given are presented in the text as facts or opinions	Place a tick in the correct column for each statement.
Give features of the text that convey information – for example, headings lists	Give short written answers.
Respond to the text – find the solutions to questions by using information in the text	Write your own views based on information from the text. There will be a number of possible answers.
Make a decision based on comparing information in different parts of the text.	Written answer. There will be no right answer, but you will need to give three reasons for your decision. Your answer and reasons must be based on information in the text.

Speaking, listening and communication

Speaking, listening and communication skills will be assessed by your teacher. You may take time ahead of your assessments to research and prepare what you want to say and you can use notes to help you on the day. You can use visual aids, if you wish.

The table below shows the tasks you will have to complete and what you should do in each case.

Type of task	Who with?	Time	You must show that you can
Discussion	About four others	About 20 minutes	Respond to information in a way that is relevant and understandable. Make contributions to the discussion using appropriate language. Take a range of roles – listening, chairing, speaking, responding, etc. Help to move the discussion forward by asking questions, summarising etc.
Presentation	On your own or as part of a small group	About 10 minutes	Present your ideas clearly. Use appropriate language. Speak persuasively. Speak appropriately for different audiences, purposes and situations.

Your writing is assessed in one 45-minute exam. There are two tasks which assess your writing skills. The total number of marks for the Writing paper is 25.

For each task, you will be given some information. You will then be given a writing task based on it. You will be told what form to write in, and you may be given some guidance on what to include.

The table below shows what you will be assessed on and what you must show you can do.

What you will be assessed on	You must show that you can
Form, communication and purpose	Use the correct format for your writing. For example, a report with headings.
	Organise your writing, using paragraphs and other features such as headings if needed.
	Include all the relevant information the reader needs, and present it clearly so that they can understand it.
	Write persuasively if you are asked to.
	Use appropriate language for the purpose.
	Write to meet the purpose. For example, to persuade or to inform.
Spelling, punctuation and grammar	Ensure your spelling and grammar are accurate and the reader can understand your meaning
	Use a range of punctuation correctly.

Top tips for success

Reading
- Make sure you answer all the questions – keep an eye on the time.
- Check the marks available for the question and the space given for your answer for a clue about how much to write.
- Read each question carefully before you look for the answer. You could highlight key words in the question so that you stay focused.
- Read the texts carefully using all your reading skills. Use skimming to work out what the text is about, scanning to find where the information you need is and close reading to find exactly the information that you need.
- Only include information taken from the right text. You will gain no marks for information from other sources.
- More than one answer might be almost right – read carefully reading to choose the one that is **exactly** right.
- Use your own words in your answers.
- If you are asked to comment on how a text is presented, say what presentation features are used **and** say how and why they are used.
- Check your answers at the end if you have time.

Speaking, listening and communication
- Prepare by researching the subject and deciding on the points you want to make.
- Be clear about your purpose and focus on achieving it.
- Be clear about your point of view and what you want to get across.
- Be clear about your audience and situation. Adjust your language to be suitable.
- Make brief notes to help you stay on track. (But don't write out a whole script.)
- Use visual aids if you want to, but don't rely on them or get distracted by the technology.
- Speak calmly, slowly and not too loudly or quietly. Make sure everyone can hear you – and make eye contact with your audience.
- Make sure you can take different roles in discussions, such as speaking, listening, chair, etc.
- When others speak, listen carefully.
- Respond politely and treat everyone's ideas as worth considering.

Writing
- Make sure you answer both questions – keep an eye on the time.
- Read the information you are given carefully.
- Read the task closely. Make sure you are clear about what writing form to use, such as briefing paper or letter.
- Show that you know and understand the features of what you are asked to write. But don't waste time laying out your writing in columns or including drawings – you will not get marks for this.
- If you are given ideas for things to include, use them.
- Write down your purpose for writing and your audience. Suit your writing to them.
- Make a quick plan to help you organise your ideas and plan paragraphs. Plan to back up your points with evidence.
- Use a range of different sentence types and connectives to link sentences.
- Check your spelling, punctuation and grammar carefully. You will lose marks for mistakes.
- Try to allow time to check your writing at the end. Correct any mistakes, and make any improvements that you can.

Section A

Read Text A and answer questions 1–6.

You have been researching teenagers' finances and have found this webpage providing information on the subject.

Text A

Teenagers get £1,000 pocket money

by Money Doctor Thursday 11 October, 2007

According to a survey by MTV One, **the average teenager now gets an allowance heading towards £1,000 a year**, with some pocketing half as much again!

Over 3,000 surveyed teenagers suggest that the term "pocket money" is not the right phrase to adequately describe the wads of cash being given to teenagers by their parents. Recently it was suggested that pocket money levels among under-16s have jumped **600%** since 1987!! **It seems that allowances rise with age with 13-year-olds getting an average of £45 a month, 16 yr olds get £80 and 18yr olds get £120!**

Most of the average annual allowance of £1,000 a year is spent on personal items such as styling products, with some spending as much as **£350**. Socialising costs slightly more across the year with teenagers spending **£360** on average; **£260** (unsurprisingly) is spent on **alcohol** and, for some, **£240 buys cigarettes**. Teenagers do love their gadgets too, with **MP3 players** and **laptops** being top of their shopping list. They also generally top up their income via gifts of around **£70 at Christmas** and **£50 on birthdays**!

But, parents, before you get too irate about teenagers just being given loads of money and not lifting their lazy little fingers, some teenagers are contributing! Over **60%** of the surveyed teenagers, including a third of those under 16, also had some sort of **paid employment**. The younger ones garden, wash cars, deliver papers and walk dogs; those over 16 do babysitting, or work in a shop or restaurant.

So, are teenagers' large allowances just a fact of life or are they just another display of over indulgent parents? *What kind of allowance do you think teenagers should get? Or should they get a job if they want an allowance?*

Why not let us know?

1 What is the **main** purpose of Text A?

....

(1 mark)

Answer questions 2 to 3 with a cross in the box [☒]. If you change your mind about an answer, put a line through the box [☒] and then mark your new answer with a cross [☒].

2 The survey found that the average amount teenagers spend on socialising is:

☐	A	£260
☐	B	£350
☐	C	£360
☐	D	£1,000

(1 mark)

3 The survey claims that the average monthly allowance for a 16 year old is:

☐	A	£60
☐	B	£80
☐	C	£120
☐	D	£1,000

(1 mark)

4 Identify **two** other sources of income for teenagers, besides pocket money, using the information in Text A.

You do **not** need to write in sentences.

i) ....

....

ii) ....

....

(2 marks)

5 Place a tick in the correct column for **each** of the six statements to show which are presented in the webpage as facts and which are opinions.

	Fact	Opinion
Many teenagers earn money through employment.		
The term 'pocket money' is unsuitable to describe the amount of money given to teenagers.		
On average, teenagers get a higher amount of pocket money as they get older.		
Under-16s today get 600% more pocket money than in 1987.		
MTV One asked more than 3,000 teenagers how much pocket money they receive.		
Teenagers who don't work make parents angry.		

(3 marks)

6 Text A claims that teenagers receive large allowances.

From your reading of the information provided, give **two** reasons why this text might be biased.

You do **not** need to write in sentences.

i) ....

....

ii) ....

....

(2 marks)

TOTAL FOR SECTION A = 10 MARKS

Section B

Read Text B and answer questions 7 – 11.

You have found this article about part-time jobs on a careers website giving advice to teenagers.

Picking the Perfect Part-Time Job

If you've got questions about finding a part-time job, read on for sensible answers and practical advice. Don't go to your next interview without them!

What is a Part-Time Job?

It is generally accepted that anything less than 35 hours per week can be considered part time.

What are the Benefits of Working Part Time?

Part-time work provides you with flexible employment that you can schedule around school and various other commitments. Working a part-time job also provides you with income and gives you work experience to put on your CV. No matter what type of job you work you will also hone the "soft skills" that all employers look for, including responsibility, independence, relationship building and time management.

What is the Pay Like for a Part-Time Job?

The pay will differ according to the type of work you do. There is no maximum amount you can earn from a part-time job, but there is a minimum wage to make sure that you are not exploited. The national minimum wage for those under the age of 18 and no longer of compulsory school age is £3.30 per hour. This jumps to £4.45 per hour when you are between the ages of 18 and 21, and to £5.35 per hour when you are aged 22 or older.

Do I Get Holidays with a Part-Time Job?

All employees, no matter how many hours per week they work, are entitled to four weeks holiday per year. You will need to ask your employer about paid bank holidays, and you will also need to ask your employer for permission before planning to take your holidays.

How Do I Get a Part-Time Job?

In order to apply for a job, create a CV and cover letter that highlight your skills and experience. A teacher or school counsellor can check this document to make sure you have formatted it correctly and included all of the relevant information. Next, look in your local papers, shop windows and notice boards for want ads. Asking contacts such as family friends or using job sites on the Internet are also good ideas. Finally, practise answering interview questions with friends and family, iron your nicest outfit and get ready to convince your interviewer that you are the best person for the job.

7 What is the main purpose of Text B?

....

(1 mark)

8 Give **three** features of Text B that help to convey information.

You do **not** need to write in sentences.

i) ....

....

ii) ....

....

iii) ....

....

(3 marks)

9 Identify **two** advantages of getting a part-time job, according to Text B.

You do **not** need to write in sentences.

i) ....

....

ii) ....

....

(2 marks)

10 According to Text B, how can a teacher help you if you are applying for a job?

You do not need to write in sentences.

....

(1 mark)

11 Your friend is considering looking for a part-time job. Which three pieces of information from Text B do you think would be most useful for your friend to know?

You do not need to write in sentences.

i) ....

....

ii) ....

....

iii) ....

....

(3 marks)

TOTAL FOR SECTION B = 10 MARKS

Section C

Read Text C and answer questions 12 – 14.

You have found three adverts for part-time jobs.

Advert 1 – online

www.bestjobs.co.uk	
Location: Firtree Business Park **Salary:** £6.00 per hour **Company:** PROTEC RECRUITMENT **Job type:** Temporary part-time jobs **Contact:** Joyce Brown	We are currently looking for Call Centre Agents to work in a busy call centre handling a high volume of incoming calls. You will have a polite and professional telephone manner with the ability to work well as part of a team. You will be expected to be available for a variety of shifts, up to 22:00 and weekends.

Advert 2 – local shop window

> LIVERY YARD in Hill Foot is looking for someone to help with general stable duties.
>
> Mornings only.
>
> Possible permanent position. 07771345678

Advert 3 – classified advert in newspaper

> ### Riverview Café
>
> – part-time staff required.
> Weekend lunchtime and evenings.
> Training given if required. Apply
> in person please at the Café at
> 21 Riverside Road, Kingham.

12 Your friend is looking for a job that won't interfere with schoolwork.

Which of the three jobs in Text C would you recommend?

Remember to give the number of the advert in your answer.

You do **not** need to write in sentences.

(1 mark)

13 A member of your family is looking for a job she can do when her young child is at nursery school.

Which of the three jobs in Text C would you recommend?

Remember to give the number of the advert in your answer.

You do **not** need to write in sentences.

(1 mark)

14 Consider the information provided in the three adverts in Text C.

Based on this information, which job would you choose to apply for?

Give three reasons.

Remember to give the number of the advert in your answer.

You do not need to write in sentences.

Job chosen ....

Reason i)   ....

Reason ii) ....

Reason iii) ....

....

....

(3 marks)

TOTAL FOR SECTION C = 5 MARKS
TOTAL FOR PAPER = 25 MARKS

Discussion

A national newspaper is sponsoring a competition for schools and colleges in which groups hold a fund-raising event for charity. There will be a £10,000 prize for the winners. The newspaper is looking for fun ideas that will raise a lot of money, and that involve as many people as possible.

In groups, discuss ideas for a fund-raising event. You should decide on one or more recommendations you could put forward to your school council, student union or tutor/supervisor.

Before the discussion, think of some interesting ideas for fund-raising activities. Try to prepare estimates of how much money could be raised by them, and how many people might be involved. If possible, collect evidence from similar events you know or can find out about. Some ideas to get you started are given below.

Need ideas that lots of people will want to join in with. Could ask friends or look on the internet?

Need to think of possible drawbacks as well as advantages – suggest how to overcome any problems.

Talent show? 'Our Town's Got Talent'. Could charge £5 per entry plus ticket sales.

Lots of people involved – judges, entrants, audience, etc. Do we need/can we get a suitable sound system?

Sponsored event? Could be fancy dress. Anyone can join in. How do we organise the sponsorship?

Quiz night? Lots of teams. Could do a raffle and sell drinks snacks, too. Who will provide the quiz questions?

Sports tournament? Could attract lots of interest – charge teams to enter and audience to watch. Have we got the facilities/equipment we need?

Presentation

A national newspaper is sponsoring a competition for schools and colleges in which groups hold a fund-raising event for charity. There will be a £10,000 prize for the winners.

You have been asked to give a presentation of your suggested fundraising idea to your school council, student union or tutor/supervisor. You should choose one idea, and brief your audience about:

- what the idea is
- how much money your idea could raise
- what roles and responsibilities would need to be taken on in organising the event
- how many people could take part in the competition if your idea is used
- how original your fund-raising activity is.

If you have completed the discussion on page 125, you may wish to draw on the ideas that were discussed, or use your own idea. Decide how much information needs to be given to everyone during the presentation. Make sure you convey your own enthusiasm for the event and can show that you have thought through all the details of what needs to be done.

There are **two** tasks which assess your writing skills.

Task 1 is worth 15 marks and Task 2 is worth 10 marks.

Remember that spelling, punctuation and grammar will be assessed in **both** tasks.

You may use a dictionary.

Task 1

Information

Your school/college has organised a car boot sale to raise money for equipment for the new Sports Hall. As a member of the school/college Council, you have received an email from the teacher in charge of organising the event.

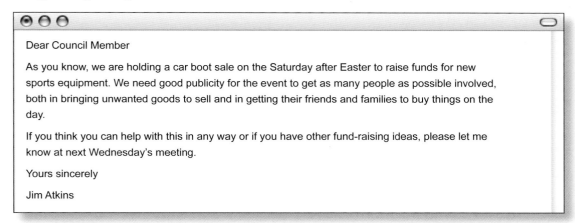

Dear Council Member

As you know, we are holding a car boot sale on the Saturday after Easter to raise funds for new sports equipment. We need good publicity for the event to get as many people as possible involved, both in bringing unwanted goods to sell and in getting their friends and families to buy things on the day.

If you think you can help with this in any way or if you have other fund-raising ideas, please let me know at next Wednesday's meeting.

Yours sincerely

Jim Atkins

Writing Task

Write an advertising leaflet for the car boot sale to persuade your fellow students to take part, making it clear why they should support this particular cause.

In your leaflet, you may include:

· details of the event taking place
· why the event has been organised and what it is hoped to achieve
· ways in which people can help

TOTAL FOR TASK 1 = 15 MARKS

Task 2

Information

You are planning to hold a 24-hour karaoke to raise extra funds for sports equipment for your school or college. You need sponsorship money to cover the costs of organising the event.

Writing Task

Write a letter to the manager of a local sports equipment suppliers asking for sponsorship for the event, making it clear why the event is happening and how the money will be spent.

Write your letter to The Manager, Top Sports (UK) Ltd., 7 Belton Way, Midthorpe, TX3 4ZT.

TOTAL FOR TASK 2 = 10 MARKS
TOTAL FOR PAPER = 25 MARKS